How to Make Divorce Fun

By Julie Collins and Trey Anderson

Published by Julie Collins and Trey Anderson

Visit us on the web at
www.howtomakedivorcefun.com

Introduction

Why is divorce so expensive? Because it's worth it!

Dedication

This book is lovingly dedicated to our ex's, as our one final insult from us to you: we say HA-HA!! This book is also dedicated to Abraham Maslow, to whom we would like to say "Thank You!" We could not have done it without you! You are our hero!

Disclaimer

This book is intended for entertainment purposes only. We realize that ex-spouses come in both genders; however, for the sake of clarity and convenience, we have used the masculine form. The authors are merely poking fun at the situation of divorce and the depths to which people will sink when faced with the inevitable demise of their nuclear family as they know it. We do not endorse the use of these strategies. Many of these strategies have been used with a high degree of success, but we do not recommend them. Names have been changed to protect the innocent and ... the not so innocent.

Preface

ANYONE WHO HAS BEEN THROUGH A DIVORCE CAN TELL YOU THAT IT IS A SAD, miserable experience. The cruelest part of divorce is that it is the death of a dream. Both parties feel angry and betrayed, and they want to lash out at the other person. This anger and animosity can be unbearably painful. The good news is that it does not have to be this way. Don't pick up that hatchet just yet. Yes, you heard us right: DIVORCE CAN BE FUN!

In order to make divorce fun, you need to accept the fact that the person you once loved and admired doesn't exist. He may have been abducted by aliens or may have been created by them. Either way he is not the person you thought you were marrying and probably never was. Let's face facts; you were played for a fool. Your ex stood at the altar and lied through his teeth, right to your face. Once you have gotten that fact through your head, the hardest part is over.

Both of the authors of this book have been divorced twice. Our experiences are similar about how awful our first divorce was, but our second divorce was only miserable until we realized that the best way to deal with the soon-to-be ex's was to PLAY WITH THEM! We developed strategies and methods to really mess with our ex's in such a way that we were no longer good victims and all our ex's wanted to do was get as far away from us as possible and as soon as possible.

There is an art to playing with your ex. This is mental chess and should be treated accordingly. It should be thought of as a game. Just be aware that it will be more comfortable to eat glass shards than to let your ex get one over on you. To be most effective, this game should last for as long as possible. Do not rush this game. Anyone can go for the throat, but we suggest that you model yourself after a cat. When a cat catches a mouse, it doesn't just rip the mouse's head off. No, the cat bats the mouse around for long periods of time. Many crafty cats will leave an opening for a mouse. The mouse will think it might be able to get away, but just before the mouse makes its escape, the cat pounces. The cat then robs the mouse of any hope. Only when the mouse is too exhausted and beaten does the cat finally break down, and, in a great show of mercy, rips its head off. The moral to the story is: Take care of your play-things; you never know when you will find another one!

CHAPTER 1

The Cruel Surprise

THE LOVE OF YOUR LIFE HAS TOLD YOU HE WANTS A DIVORCE. OH NO! WE know how bad this hurts. Let's face it, you are being rejected. We have heard several excuses of why a person leaves. One of the most popular reasons is, "I love you but I am not 'IN' love with you." Now you may be asking yourself, "What the fuck does that mean?" Well, it means that they have the emotional maturity of a junior high school adolescent; they recognize love as infatuation, not a state of being. They are not emotionally mature enough to recognize that love is not the hundred-yard dash, but a long journey that was meant to last a lifetime. These people are emotional vampires that have been sucking you dry; now that they are done, they are ready to move on to their next victim!

Another popular reason is, "I do not love you anymore." Ouch, can you think of anything more cruel to say to someone? Or worse yet, can you imagine having someone tell you this on your birthday, or in an anniversary card? The truth of the matter is that they never loved you at all. Their hearts were never involved. They were playing you. Sorry!

The third excuse that seems to be popular is, "I have fallen in love with someone else." These are all painful. They all have a way of making you analyze what you may have done to cause this. What could you have done differently to make things better or to make them want to stay? There are three simple questions you need to answer to learn if you are indeed an evil person who deserves what is happening to you. They are as follows:

1. Are you cheating?
   No) Go get yourself a good massage
   Yes) Sign up for a frontal lobotomy
2. Do you suffer with a mental illness or are you involved with drugs?
   No) Eat extra chocolate
   Yes) Have yourself committed at some place that will give you a frontal lobotomy
3. Are you abusive?
   No) Take a weekend vacation
   Yes) Seriously consider suicide as a community service

If the answer to all of these is no, then you are the victim of cruel circumstance, which is the main reason this handy-dandy divorce manual needed to be written. Together, we will show you how not to be a Qua-Qua victim, but a Ha-Ha survivor!

There are several strategies that must be mastered to be the Ha-Ha survivor. We will go into the details of these strategies in later chapters, but briefly: get over your ex, make them a joke, destroy their self-esteem, and annihilate their sense of security. In the meantime, you will maintain your "good guy" image.

Who We Are
Why We Are the Experts

Both of the authors of this book have been divorced twice. Most of our friends are divorced. It is pretty common for us to meet a jilted lover who is going through a divorce, boo-hoo-ing about how hurt she is. We have spent many hours discussing tactics and strategies to help our friends deal with their ex's. Occasionally, we meet someone new who has not figured out how to go about divorcing her spouse without losing half of her stuff, or who is allowing her soon-to-be ex to make life miserable with both legal and mind games.

We are very indulgent with these people. We will listen to their sad sob stories for all of 60 seconds before we tell them that they have a choice. They can continue to play victim to their ex's vile temperament, or they can become someone that their ex does not want to mess with. It is their choice. If you are going through a divorce from the standpoint of the person refusing to be abused, we will get drunk with you and spend the night laughing and helping you to plot against your ex. We do not even charge for this service because it is so much FUN! However, if you are approaching this situation as the victim, we will get you drunk and take notes of how skillfully your ex is playing you. Then, once you leave, we will spend the night laughing at you and getting drunk without you, so that we are prepared to rake your stupid ass over the coals the next time we see you. Hell, we may even call your ex, and congratulate him on what a fine job he is doing. If you want sympathy, get a shrink or a support group. We have heard you can find sympathy between shit and syphilis; check Webster's. We are not your best bet.

There are always choices in life. There are two ways you can end this "thing." The most important step you can take is to remember that this is a temporary situation. You may hold your head high and handle this time with grace and dignity. Or, you can lose control and spew hate and pain to everyone around you. You can whine and cry until everyone in your vicinity cringes when you open your mouth. Is that how you get what you want? We hope not.

If you choose the former, we can help you. If you insist on taking the latter, our philosophies will not apply to your self-imposed prison. We will suggest some very simple techniques that will simplify your situation and spare you from embarrassing yourself. You need to ask yourself some really tough questions. You may not even need a divorce. We'll help you decide when you've had enough. How do you know when to walk away?

Marriage is the most important business investment you will make in your entire life. Some of us were too lax in choosing our spouses in the first place. Others chose carefully only to find out that their spouses horribly misrepresented themselves. Finally, the worst reason ever for getting married: "I had to." Whether knocked up, indicted, or trapped, it never works out when you look at marriage as an obligation. Whatever the case may be in your situation, the end result is always the same: Divorce. Sorry!

We're not big proponents of a huge amount of risk; however, in order to get ahead, you have to roll the dice. As far as choosing a partner, we're the last people on the planet to ask. We'd just like to say for the record that there is absolutely no room for error when choosing a mate. Even when the whole deal looks golden, you can still screw up. We're just the best people to tell you when to walk out; it's our specialty. We can talk until we're blue in the face about how to choose a mate; however, if that's the market you're in, boy, did you buy the wrong book!

"No-fault divorce" not only sucks, but it is a lie! It is always someone's fault. There are three reasons to file for divorce. "I changed my mind," or "I need to find myself," are not reasons, they are excuses. Even "I'm gay," doesn't let you off the hook. You should have known about that before you took your vows. You're probably not gay, just greedy. If you hit it once, it can't be that bad. Buck up and live with it. It's no reason to ruin a family: just don't screw around on your spouse. It's far too dangerous with the plethora of venereal diseases out there. Wouldn't it suck if your spouse gave you AIDS or some other horrible disease that will drain your children's trust fund before it will let you die?

This brings us to the first deal breaker. Cheating! If you cheated or if you married a cheater, throw in the towel. You will never get over it and neither will your mate. It will always be there, no matter what you do. It doesn't matter why it happened; it doesn't even really matter where or who. What counts is that it did happen, and you need to retain an attorney immediately. Of course, with no-fault divorce, you'll still pay out the ass, but it is always better to end it sooner rather than later. Otherwise, you will spend the rest of your life fearful of when it will happen again, or resenting and torturing your spouse for something he did to you 10 years ago. Either way, you're scared or you will become a nag, so it's best just to walk away and torture your wretched ex from afar.

If you were the one that cheated and you got away with it, for the love of God, Don't Ever Confess. Thank your lucky stars that you got away with it and promise yourself it will never happen again. THEN NEVER EVER DO IT AGAIN!!! You deserve to have to live life everyday knowing what you did. The most selfish thing you can do is dump it on your blissfully unaware partner. If you want to get caught, get caught and get out; it's kindest to everyone involved.

The second reason to get out is abuse. Be it physical or verbal, there is no excuse for it. If you are being abused and it happens more than once, you're at fault too. If you are the abuser, why in the hell would you want to be involved with a doormat? You can't respect yourself or your partner if abuse (either physical or mental) is part of your relationship dynamic. If your spouse is a bully or if you are a punching bag, someone needs to rally the brain cells and get the hell out before one of you winds up dead or serving life without parole.

Abuse is confusing. There are people who whine constantly and need their asses kicked. If their parents didn't raise them right, then you shouldn't be married to them in the first place. On the other hand, hitting, name calling, and damaging property should be considered abuse and someone needs to hit the bricks. Everyone is going to fight, but you need to fight fair. Unless you can keep it above the belt, divorce is on the horizon.

The third reason (and our favorite deal breaker) is addiction. It can be drugs, alcohol, work, or sex (not with your spouse, ask Hillary). There is no way you can live with someone who suffers from addiction. They're so fucked up it is best if you just run them off. Leave them to their addiction; they love it more than you anyway. If you are a glutton for punishment, you can stick around and try to help, but you're more of a hindrance because you're too close to the situation to be of any good to anyone, especially yourself. We are friends with a lot of "addictive" people but that's where it has got to stop. These people can't care about anyone else because they don't even give a damn about themselves.

These are called "deal breakers" for a reason. There is a 99.9 percent chance of the offender repeating the offense. If you feel you need or deserve to go through this horrible thing every 5 to 7 years, by all means enjoy your existence as a victim, get neutered, and quit whining so the rest of us can get on with our lives! We don't want to hear about it all the time.

Be honest with yourself when considering divorce. If you have one or more of the three deal breakers, you can try whatever you want, but it's not going to work out. No need to take our word for it. Go ahead and try—no skin off our noses! No matter what you do, or how hard you try, you'll wind up in divorce court sooner or later. It's always better sooner, because it's cheaper and less painful, believe it or not. You need to do some serious soul searching when making your decision because there is no going back once you have made up your mind. If your spouse made up your mind for you, you're still screwed. Just keep a stiff upper lip and get through it the best you can. Acceptance is where you need to have your head at this point.

This is where our first making divorce fun tip comes in. Never utter, whisper, speak or yell your ex's name again. Ever. You must strike it from your vocabulary right now. Once you have a deal breaker their name is to never be spoken by you again, unless the judge makes you say it. You may be wondering how exactly that can be accomplished. It's actually very easy. When your children are present you must refer to the ex as "Your Mother" or "Your Father" this implies that the poor child is stuck with this idiot as a relation forever, you on the other hand are off the hook.

When your children are not present is when the fun begins! Since you'll no longer be using the ex's given name you must come up with something for use in conversation. You must completely dehumanize the ex and the best way to start your divorce is with a nickname. Think back: When you first got together, the idiot deserved a name, probably "cupcake," or something equally as nauseating. Now you get to hand down the name he deserves. Be as creative as you can! I used to refer to my ex as the "bastard," until there were two. Now I just refer to them as "Defendant A and Defendant B". Actually, I really don't refer to them at all unless prompted by some well meaning press person. When someone comes to tell me "ex news!" (GAG) and refers to them by their given name it actually takes me a moment to realize who they may be referring to. By coming up with a "special" name for him you have taken the first step towards your new independence. Please, be honest and personal when you make this up; if you're lucky you'll get to call it to his face before this whole mess is over. Try to draw on something that refers to their less than stellar moral character (Mommy Dearest) or his lack of bedroom desire (two-pump chump) or their hygiene or looks (Dirty Hippie). Make sure everyone you know uses it in a sentence and you're in business!

The whole situation is tragic and needs to be treated as such. Divorce and death have too much in common. If your dog, mom, or dad died, you wouldn't be expected to just brush it off and be fine the next day. Divorce is the same way. We take divorce for granted in our society and that really sucks. Don't push yourself too hard at first.

Give yourself a break, and if there are some days when you just can't cope, then don't. This is war and if you go in weak, you're going to lose. You've got to have your head straight and never, never let emotion get involved, at least if the sun is up. This is strictly a business situation and you need to be able to treat it as such. Be a hard ass. Never back down unless you have no other options. They may whine and bawl but you need to be immune to it. So many times intelligent people wind up going back for the same thing over and over. Stay strong no matter what. You are doing the right thing, it doesn't matter how bad it gets. It's kind of like childbirth: You really, really want it over as soon as possible, and you don't want to repeat it anytime soon.

If your spouse is the one who had papers served on you, that bites. Be honest with yourself—you saw it coming. He might have been overly nice or incredibly distant. Don't act like a dumb ass and pretend you didn't see it coming. We know of an ex-husband who was flabbergasted when his wife reminded him that they wouldn't be having lunch on Monday because she was moving out. She told him 6 months previously that if things didn't change, she was going to leave. He must not have heard her. It wasn't her fault—another 6 months of being thrown under the bus and she was more than ready to go. Her only regret was that she did not change the locks and kick him out on his ass; it would've been a hell of a lot easier and cheaper in the long run. The wife of this story had learned her lesson. When the woman's second husband, the narcissist, suffered a psychotic episode, he was shocked to discover that his keys never worked again. Like we said, it gets easier each time you get divorced. Practice makes perfect.

Don't stay because of lame excuses. "I need the money" doesn't count because this is the age of equal rights. We do not agree with that crap. Now you will have to clean the house, cook the food, do the laundry, buy the groceries, and pay the mortgage. You will also be in charge of vehicle maintenance, yard work, and all the other outside jobs God invented. It can be done. We've done it alone with no assistance for 10 years. We don't have a college education or a trust fund. We also have never spent a day on welfare or on any federal or state assistance. No one has missed any meals either. You can retain your self respect and dignity with hardly any help. Don't ruin yourself for an extra paycheck.

On the up-side, you can decide where you want to spend your money, who and what you want to spend it on, and no one will ever bitch at you about anything. If the dog gets too lippy, you can always have him put down. Independence is entirely underrated. Taking no crap is priceless.

Another bad excuse to keep a horrible marriage is for religious beliefs. Even Catholics will let you off the hook for the right reasons. Pride is important, but divorce just doesn't have the social stigma it had 30 years ago. There is nothing wrong with knowing when to walk away from a bad investment. If it gets to the point where you're dealing with any of the aforementioned issues, it's time to walk away. Give yourself some hope and a new life because the one you have now is a dead end. It will end badly for everyone involved.

Habit is comfortable, but it's just an existence. You have a choice to go out and experience life to its fullest, or you can merely exist with an anchor around your neck. You will eventually drown in the familiar. This will stunt your life, and you will pass up the chance to learn and grow.

Many people will tough out a marriage because of the kids. Give me a break! How are your kids supposed to learn about a good marriage if you don't have one? In this day of instant gratification, divorce has devastated the majority of families, so your kids will fit right in. They'll handle it as well as you do. When we were growing up in the (gulp) 1970's, everyone had two parents. Julie never knew she had it tough until she was in her 20's and someone actually felt sorry for her. Julie was confused. Her mother was a feminist; she actually drove a women's rights float in the Idaho Falls (Mormonville) Parade in 1972. Needless to say, she didn't need no stinking man. So she didn't have one. She was married to the entirely too-good-looking party guy. Bad choice: She's still pissed about it 30 years later.

A very valuable lesson for everyone is when you're done, walk away and let it go. If you have enough guts, you can do it. Even if you pretend you have enough guts, you can do it. We're not encouraging anyone to go it alone if you don't have to. But if you're in a crappy situation, for the love of God, get out. It's scary and uncomfortable, but so is being married to the wrong person. Change is the most important part of the human experience, but we almost always fight it. But if we don't change, then we are as good as dead.

CHAPTER 2

The Facts of Life, Take Care of Yourself

Maslow

Once upon a time, there was a man named Abraham Maslow, who in 1943 wrote a psychology paper called "A Theory of Human Motivation." What Abraham did not realize is that what he wrote was the Holy Grail of how to really fuck with your ex's world. You will be using the "Theory of Human Motivation" as a guide to making yourself stronger and at the same time reducing your ex to a quivering paranoid psychotic. While Abraham Maslow was trying to understand what motivates people to act, what he really discovered was the recipe to winning your divorce. We will define this further in the next chapter, but before getting to that, we can demonstrate to your ex that you can take away his security and comfort. Subsequently, this will increase his desire to GET AWAY from you! We need to know what makes him tick. This is important to understand because each action you take should somehow relate to Maslow's theory. When in doubt, all you have to do is ask yourself, "What would Maslow do?"

Maslow believed that people have needs in order to be happy and content. He believed that these needs had to be satisfied by order of priority before a person could move on to the next level of needs. These needs are physiological, safety, social, esteem, and self-actualization.

Physiological Needs

These needs include excreting, eating, drinking, sleeping, acquiring shelter, and staying warm. Ok, it is not feasible for you to keep your ex's from eating and drinking, unless you kidnap them and lock them in the closet. Then they get loose, call the police, and the next thing you know—you are sitting in the pokey getting pokeyed by some big hairy guy who has taken to referring to you as "his bitch." No good for you! You cannot keep them from excreting unless you kill them, but then if you get caught, you are right back to being the big hairy guy's bitch. It's still not good for you. Messing with their sleep and possibly shelter can be done without too much risk of becoming Bubba's bitch.

Safety Needs

Safety needs are feelings of security. Do you have a job? Are you making enough money? Can you pay rent? Can you afford to take you or

your kids to a doctor if you need to? Are you safe from crime? These are your primary goals. You must have these goals satisfied before you can truly play your ex with finesse. You need to ask yourself a few simple questions about the ex. Can you get your ex fired anonymously? (Or even not so anonymously, it's always fun to take credit for your work.) If your ex has used his position at a job to commit a crime, such as telling the world confidential information (at a law firm, for example), then turn him in for that crime. It is the right thing to do, after all, and you will be doing the world a service! People will actually think you're honorable. Can you get him kicked out of his apartment/house? What can you do to cause your ex sleepless nights?

Social Needs

After physiological needs and safety needs are met and satisfied, a person will begin to build a social network, reconnect with old friends, make more friends, find a new lover, and network with family. If your ex is female, you may think that she is trying to satisfy this need before satisfying the safety needs. It is pretty common for a woman (and some men) to move in with a new lover immediately after a divorce. What they are actually doing is trading sex for security. Since no one likes to think of themselves as a whore, your ex probably has not even admitted the reality of what he is doing, even to himself. Educate him! Let him know they are not only a whore, but a cheap whore. Oh, and if you are male and can step into a situation where you can move a girl in for sex, giving her a little security and possibly some shelter is really some pretty cheap entertainment! Besides, if she is no good at it, you can always kick her slutty ass out!

Esteem Needs

We all want to feel that we matter and that we count. We need to have high self-esteem and to feel that we are valued by our associates, friends, and family. In fact, if you were to take an honest look at yourself, you would probably realize the reason that you are so mad at your ex is because he has denied you respect and acceptance. The truth of the matter is that you feel like you have been thrown away and treated like a used Kleenex. It was certainly important for you to be there when he was excreting snot from his nose, but now that you are full of snot, you are no longer of any value to him so he throws you away. DAMN HIM!!!

Don't worry, with the help of this book, you will teach him lessons he will never forget. Take note of how badly you are hurting at this point. Remember this feeling while you are chiseling away at your ex's psyche and sense of security.

Self-Actualization

The sooner you can reach this stage, the better off you are. This is the stage where your ex does not have any real hold on you. All your needs are met and you are free to start plotting your revenge. Treat you like a worthless piece of used tissue, will he? Yeah, we will cut off his nose just to spite his face! HA-HA!

This is the mindset you have to be in to be truly effective at playing the divorce game. It is so much easier to come up with cool and fun surprises when you are not worrying about money, laundry, kids, or security. Make it your goal to have a social life that is happy and fulfilled. When you have surrounded yourself with true friends who not only want to help you plot against your ex, but actually enjoy the company you provide, you have arrived! They will enjoy hearing how you have turned your ex into a joke. If you can reach this level, you will win the game of divorce.

CHAPTER 3

Recuperating from Divorce Will Resemble an AA Program

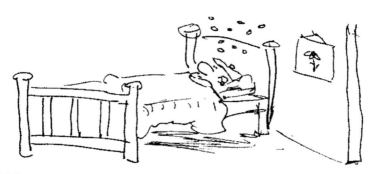

W E ARE NOT PSYCHOLOGISTS, BUT EVEN WE POOR SIMPLE LAYMEN REALIZE that you have got to take care of yourself, period. End of report. You must reach the self-actualizing stage before you can plot effectively. Divorce hurts ... a lot. It is so damn painful that you would not wish this kind of emotional stress on your worst enemy. Well, maybe your worst enemy, but no one else. The person you trusted most in the whole world just stomped a hole in your guts with no remorse. It's normal to want him to pay for it.

This is where the big secret comes in. The best revenge you can have is living well. Nothing is more annoying to the person who just threw you away than to discover that not only are you a valuable commodity, but that you are better off without them. How in the hell is that supposed to happen when you can barely get out of bed and the constant ache won't go away? Simple: Let it run its course. Depression is like the flu or a nasty cold. You cannot have the 24-hour bug without going through 24 hours of hell.

Divorce is the same thing. Unfortunately, it lasts a hell of a lot longer than 24 hours. It's up to you to decide how long you're willing to spend on it. Some of us drink, have sex with strangers, or any other myriad of self-destructive behaviors, just to wake up and find we're still not over it. For some people, this can go on for years. They act like everything is just great, but they still can't stop talking or thinking about the ex. Keep in mind that depression is just anger without the enthusiasm.

There are some simple steps you can follow that will allow you to get on with your life. It's all about our behavior and accepting those things that we cannot change. YIKES, this is sounding and smelling suspiciously like an AA meeting. Who knows, maybe they have something there. However, our 12 steps don't require letter writing or meetings and are a hell of a lot more fun!

1. GET REALLY SHIT-FACED SLOBBERING DRUNK. We're talking so drunk you have to hold on to the carpet so you don't fall off. Not an Alcoholics Anonymous recommended action, but therapeutic. This shouldn't go on for more than 3 or 4 days.

2. CRY. Crying is always done best when hung over. That way you kill two birds with one stone. It hurts. It's kind of like popping a zit. You've got to get the poison out. Don't forget the Kleenex. It's important to plan. We're notoriously cheap and don't stock Kleenex. If you're going to bawl, Kleenex is required. Toilet paper will leave a mark. Your face will thank you later. This shouldn't take longer than 24 hours. If you need longer than that, you may have caused permanent liver damage during phase 1. Please

remember that crying must be done solo. If you involve your friends and cohorts, they'll just try to cheer you up, which is the last thing you need at this point. Our advice is Wallow, Wallow, Wallow. Divorce is like death. Take the time to mourn your loss. Grieving is important and shouldn't be overlooked.

3. CLEAN YOUR HOUSE. This accomplishes a couple of things. It gets the stale aura of your ex out of your space, and let's be realistic; you've been drunk and bawling for a week, it's time to clean house. Get on with it. Start taking care of business—the serious business of teaching your ex that no one treats you like this and gets away with it.

4. CRASH-DIET TIME. God has a great sense of humor. There are some people who eat constantly when they are depressed and there are others who eat hardly anything. In case you are the type that eats a lot when depressed, we suggest only keeping food in the house that takes time to prepare. You are depressed. You really are not going to feel like cooking. Maybe you should take up smoking. If you are the type that hardly eats anything, then thank your lucky stars. This is the "Divorce Diet." It is God's way of making you HOT again!!! If Jenny Craig could bottle this shit, she'd rule the world. There is nothing better than facing your ex—15 pounds lighter. Let's face it, you've just shed 205 (or however much he weighed) unwanted toxic pounds, what's another 10 pounds or so?

5. NEW CLOTHES. Fuck it, even if you don't have the money, indulge a little. Find a trendy thrift store if you must. A massage, manicure, pedicure, facial, and new hairdo will fix anything. Investing time and money into yourself is a great way of telling the world that you are worth it! It will also make facing your new cruel world a little easier. This is your equivalent of war paint and armor. You'll need it because you're going into battle!

6. PUT ON YOUR GAME FACE. Make a decision that no matter what you will face, don't ever let others see you cry. Practice smiling and nodding. Never give anyone the power to ruffle you.

They aren't worth fucking up your contacts or, God forbid, your eyeliner.

7. GO OUT AND TROLL FOR ASS. Call up your single friends. They are still there and if you followed our advice, they will still hang out with you. This is not as much about getting laid, as it is about having a good time with your friends, checking out what is available in members of the opposite sex, and possibly finding someone you can talk to.

   Choose someone who does not know your ex and will tell you what a groovy person you are. Practice pool, then kick ass on whoever is dumb enough to try and take your money. I know what I'm talking about; I had a pool table installed in my living room. Breaking up is an art. Do not lower your standards. The good news is: The more often you do it, the easier it gets. Hell, you can get down to your high school weight. Yea!! The most important part of this is DO NOT lower your standards. Don't get drunk and do something dumb you'll feel bad about later. Hopefully, you came equipped with a good eject button. Just remember that spending the night puking on the bathroom floor is better than sleeping with someone who is going to require limb removal just to get out of their lair. Keep in mind that it is dark in the bar and you can miss important details, such as nasty ear hair, unfortunate moles that are misplaced, and God knows what else. This is why God invented St. Bernards and Doritos.

8. GET LAID. Yep, you've graduated, sort of. Our philosophy (from a pair that has lots of heartbreak under our belts) is that the best way to get over someone is to get under someone else as soon as possible. Just watch out; they may stick around. There are several rules about casual recreational sex that MUST be observed. The first thing to remember is that you are recreating, not procreating. For God's sake, do not bring a child into a single-parent situation. The world can always use one less bastard. The other thought to consider is to do no harm (yes, this includes emotional harm).

19

Before you start fucking like little rabbits, let your partner know that you are not emotionally involved, that you just want to be held and enjoy the comfort that sex brings. Do not lead your partner into thinking that there is a possibility for more. Do not treat him the way your ex has treated you. Finally, you need to be take care of protection. God created latex for a reason. You think your sex life sucks now, try navigating it with a bad case of herpes or worse! In Julie's experience, her "one night stands" have a shelf life of about 2 years. Then 2 years later, when they still don't love her back, she then feels like an ass and starts over again at step 1. She's just grateful she gets to do it with all her stuff, because she's learned that Divorce SUX! The most important thing to keep in mind is that sleeping with someone with the sole intent of getting over someone else is an art.

Never try it with someone you actually know and kind of like or even don't care that much for, as it will never work. Go somewhere you never go. Try to find someone you find physically appealing but doesn't have a lot to talk about. If you're really lucky, you can find someone who is nice to look at but isn't too bright. Never divulge your real name (if the ex has a new lover, borrow his name). Never take them to your house; this encourages that pesky stalking thing. Most important, do not, and we repeat, DO NOT stay the night. A friend of ours once told us that when we sleep together (not hot monkey sex, but real REM sleep), our souls bond and at this point who can afford that? You'll be doing well just to keep yourself together without your subconscious sabotaging you into thinking that you really like this brainless chimp you have chosen to fulfill your physical void. GO HOME!

9. TAKE A BREAK. It's ok if you want to take a hiatus. Julie did for years. She learned sex and cigarettes are real similar. The longer you go without, the easier it is. You still crave it, but the craving gets less and less with each passing day. Hell, after 6 months you won't even remember what it looks like. But you'll still crave it.

Back to that damn human condition. We're all required to have touch. How pathetic is that? Just take everything as it comes, and don't forget that this too will pass. You can take a fuck buddy if it fits into your thing. Julie doesn't do it because it goes against her policy. She tries to avoid fucking anyone she either likes or respects. Who in the hell can afford losing a good friend for the sake of sex? It just ain't worth it. Friends of the opposite sex are great. Most of the time they are best left as just friends.

10. PLAN YOUR DIVORCE PARTY. This is the best! You don't have to make your friends dress up like idiots and there is a chance for guilt-free sex. Once again, we can't stress this part enough: God invented latex for this purpose. She (God) may have a wicked sense of humor but She has our best interest at heart in the long run. Don't question too much. There is a master plan; if we knew what it was we probably wouldn't want to play. There needs to be lots of food and lots of booze. Invite all your single friends and maybe a few of your cool, supportive married friends. Everyone needs to understand that it's like a wake: the end of an era and the dawning of a new one (albeit a lonely and depressing era, but a new one nonetheless). Best to make the most of it.

11. GET A DOG. Cats are sort of cool if you don't need to depend on them for anything and do not mind having a box of SHIT in your house! But there is nothing better than a canine pal. They won't fuck your sister or run up your credit cards. You can have them neutered or spayed and they don't really care all that much. They won't lecture you about your drinking, and they'll never tell you that your new pants make your ass look huge.

Julie has a St. Bernard named Marc. He is named after the guy that she was horribly infatuated with, until Trey pointed out that he had an abnormally large head. She later learned that he had sex with his sister. (The guy, not Marc!)

This trick of naming your pet after "the one that got away" works like a charm. Marc is listed first in the phone book so when one of those pesky telemarketers call and asks for Marc, she says yeah, he's here, hang on. He's pre-approved for all kinds of credit cards and vehicle loans. He's spoiled rotten and neurotic, but he's all hers. He makes big dents in her house, he smells bad, he drools and eats a whole bunch, but he loves her like she loves him. Unconditionally. He keeps her safe and he sleeps with her no matter what. EWWW. Soul bonding with a drool monster!?

The best part about Julie's Marc is that he has replaced what's-his-name and now she doesn't even have to think of that guy ever. What's-his-name has big ears, a huge head, and had sex with his sister! Trey just thought he would remind her AGAIN!!!! Just a tip to you single people; find someone with a real dog (anything that weighs less than 8 pounds isn't really a dog) and see how they treat their pet. It's just how they'll treat you, if you prove yourself worthy. Don't fuck up.

12. ACCEPT YOUR FATE. Hope springs eternal, right? Not really, but if you can find peace with yourself, nothing else matters. Just keep in mind that the person you married has his own issues and you don't need any of those. As long as you can sleep at night and know you did everything in your power to make things work, it's on them. Grandma Rose always said it takes two. Grandma Rose was wrong. It may take two to have a marriage, but it only takes one to destroy it. So let's teach him a lesson! If you refuse to let your ex get the best of you, you win in the long run. Isn't that what it's all about anyway?

These steps are easy compared to what alcoholics have to go through. The most important thing is that there are no meetings to attend or embarrassing letters to write.

CHAPTER 4

The Players and the Game

Playing the Field

There are five groups of people that are involved in your game of divorce. They are you, your ex, your children, your attorney, and your spies. The goal of successful divorcing is to climb up Maslow's hierarchy of needs while systematically preventing your ex from doing the same. The first one to the top will be called the Ha-Ha ex and the one that does not quite make it will be called the Qua-Qua ex. We will explain these two terms in greater detail shortly.

The third players on the divorce field are your children. This is really an unfortunate situation. Children have no business being in the middle of divorce, but due to the nature of divorce, the children are the ultimate losers. Both you and your ex should actively work to keep your children out of divorce.

The fourth player is your attorney. Attorneys can be very damaging unless both parties have one. Then they seem to cancel each other out. Always get your own attorney. There is a name for the person who walks into a court room without an attorney, or God forbid shares one. They are called "THE LOSER."

The fifth players are your spies. They need to be handled with the utmost care and respect. They will make you or break you.

The Dick and Jane Story

There are two kinds of people in this world: the victimizers and the victims. Everyone becomes a victim at some point in life, either through ignorance or just plain trusting the wrong people. It is what you do afterward that defines who you are.

If you are the kind of person who holds your head high and takes the emotional abuse, refusing to lower yourself to "their" level, we respectfully have dubbed you the Qua-Qua. This title is to honor a doormat named Dick. Dick was very happily married to a wonderfully creative manipulator. Being in love, Dick did not see that he was, in fact, married to an evil genius.

After their separation, Dick's ex hatched an insidious plot to make Dick look like a fool. Viciously attacking his self-esteem, she forced Dick to move down a level on Maslow's chart. Dick was so in love with his ex-wife, he did not even see it coming. Dick made the tragic error in judgment that if he were nice enough and kind enough to her, she would take pity on how pathetic he is and ask him to come home. Jane, Dick's ex, smelled his weakness, and like a predator with smell of blood in her nostrils, she attacked.

She convinced him that he was the worst father on the planet. Even though he had been serving our country in Iraq, she ruthlessly tore his esteem and psyche to shreds. Dick was at fault for his situation as he allowed her to convince him that he was the worst father in the history of the planet. He was willing to agree to anything. She guilt-tripped him about their daughter's education. In his desperation to fix his family and prove to his ex that he was willing to do whatever it took to patch it up, he very effectively showed this predator his jugular. Jane told him that if he were truly interested in taking an active role, he needed to attend a school function. There was a parent-teacher seminar taking place. The whole idea of this seminar, she said, was to let the parents experience what the children were doing in class.

Dick enthusiastically attended the seminar. In the seminar all the other "parents" were practicing their handwriting and learning phonic skills. Dick, along with the other "parents," learned that QU makes a QUA sound. After about an hour with no mention of children or curriculum, Dick's heart began to let loose and his brain started to guide his actions. Dick finally asked himself, "What is going on here?" So Dick asked the instructor what kind of seminar this was exactly. The instructor very patiently explained in small terms to Dick that he was attending a remedial writing class for illiterate adults. Dick took his college education and his neatly printed worksheets and went to visit his good friend whose shoulder he had been crying on for months.

He proceeded to explain what happened at this seminar that he had been looking so forward to attending. After 45 minutes of raucous laughter, his friend wiped the tears from her eyes, looked Dick in the face, and said QUA-QUA! So in your honor, Dick, we have dubbed the victims as quaquas. It should be noted that Dick whined incessantly in true Qua-Qua manner until everyone who knew him would cringe and make fun of the Jane report that they received daily for years. Even though we had some really great betting pools and won some good money from his horrible plight and consistently bad decisions, we really could have done without his incessant whining and crying. However, we usually found the Jane report highly entertaining.

No one knows whatever became of Dick. It is rumored that he moved away and began a compound in the mountains of Northern

Idaho. It's called Qua-Quaville. The moral to the story is that taking the high road will lead you to Qua-Quaville. Be willing to get your hands dirty, and you will do all right.

We would like to commend Jane on her creative twist in the whole proceeding. She has been a great inspiration in the writing of this book. In her honor we have compiled a list of entertaining places you can invite your ex. This can be fun-to-do-at-school functions, or family gatherings, or any other social situation where a slightly raised "whisper" will create a ton of amusing gossip about them.

ENTERTAINING PLACES TO INVITE YOUR EX

Adult illiteracy class

Alcoholic Anonymous meetings

Poetry readings (pick a weird one at a local coffee shop)

Amway seminars

Anger management class

Sex-aholics Anonymous gatherings

V.D. support groups

Parenting class

Battered women support groups (for him)

Mary Kay facial parties

Tupperware parties

Any place where there are other unstable adults whining about anything and everything.

Remember, the point of this exercise is to introduce your ex into a new subculture of people who think they have it REALLY bad. Hopefully, they will fall into a "poor me" rut and open themselves up for a brutal victimization orchestrated by you.

Qua-Qua aka "The Victims"

This is what you are trying so desperately to avoid becoming. They are the people who gain the most weight, age horrifically, and had to buy all new furniture. The Qua-Qua will still be incessantly crying and whining long after the ink has dried. This will cause their friends and family to hate them. Eventually they are forced to move to Idaho and join the compound lovingly referred to as Qua-Quaville.

Ha-Ha aka "The Winners"

If Qua-Qua's are victims, then Ha-Ha's must be the victimizers.

Being the Ha-Ha starts with one simple idea: "The shit is mine and I am going to fuck with you until you walk away! I am going to create problems in your life, lie to you, and mislead you. I am going to find ways to cost you lots of money. I am going to make you feel insecure, and I am going to attack your self-esteem and make you look either crazy or foolish every single chance I get. I will keep going until you agree to go away with what is fair, not what you feel you are entitled to because you are mad and want to knock me down as low as you can!" Ha-Ha's are easily identified by their catch phrase of "HA-HA." Ha-Ha's have all the power and are going to pick their battles and win the war. It is up to the Ha-Ha to take what is theirs.

The Ha-Ha's goal is to get rid of the ex without buying them off, not to take all the Qua-Qua's stuff. Be fair with your ex. There will be several times during this hurtful period of your life that your ex will accuse you of things that you did not do. There will also be times when your ex accuses you of things you did do. Regardless of whether or not you did do the evil, vile deed you are being accused of, just point your finger at your ex and say "HA-HA." Listen to your ex's; if they accuse you of doing something you did not do, it means that you should immediately do whatever they accused you of (if you can get away with it while retaining a clean criminal record). Don't get caught.

It is a good idea to always keep your ex's on the extremes of under-estimating you or overestimating you. If they underestimate you, then they are open for a brutal victimization; if they overestimate you, then they are spending all of their time trying to guess what you will do next and not try to attack you! If they can get to a point where they feel secure, they will move up Maslow's chart and then they will be one step closer to winning the game. Keep them in Qua-Quaville with Dick. Do whatever it takes to cause them lots of sleepless nights.

CHAPTER 5

Asshole

You need to find the nastiest divorce lawyer available. The best way to go about this is to check references. Think of your friends; after all, you're not the first person to be in this predicament. Try to remember the person you felt the sorriest for ever. You know the person who had their ass handed to them on a platter. Call them and find out who exactly represented their ex. Retain that attorney immediately. It is always best to learn from other people's mistakes rather than having them learn from yours.

If you don't follow that one simple step, you will wind up with a geriatric woman as an attorney who can't spell, and then you are totally screwed.

We would be doing you a huge disservice if we did not explain the anatomy of the divorce attorney. If you depend on your attorney to fight all your battles, you will wind up spending far too much money and will lose your ass. Speaking of asses, the best analogy we could come up with is, your attorney is your asshole. You pay him to remove the shit from your life. As we have all experienced constipation, it is important to remember to chew your food (ex) thoroughly before passing it on to your rectum. This will make the entire experience as comfortable and as cheap as possible.

Picking an attorney is one of the most important parts of getting a divorce. Your attorney's job is to protect you and to look out for your best interests. Sometimes it will seem to you that your attorney is being too harsh with your ex. Do not worry, that is what you are paying him to do. Much of the time your attorney will go for your ex's jugular so that they have some negotiating room to "compromise on." Let your attorney do the job that you hired him for. No matter what the situation you have hired an attorney to handle, the bigger asshole he is, the more bang you are getting for your buck. Unfortunately, lawyers also play golf together and if one of his other clients has more money than you do and is getting a divorce at the same time, it could spell trouble for you. If your lawyer is out with someone else's lawyer there is no guarantee that your life won't be used as a pawn on the fourth green. Take care of your own business and stay on top of every little detail.

The more leg work you can do yourself, the more money you will save in the long run. Hopefully, once you have totally decimated your ex, he will not only be willing, but begging to settle, so you'll be able to avoid the entire nastiness of a hearing.

Watch out for mediators. They are not on your side, and do not let them talk you into giving up what is rightfully yours. The mediation process is a bunch of shit. It is designed to let the legal system off the hook. Usually, the person who is the most reasonable and realistic is the one who takes it in the shorts. Go to mediation completely emotional and irrational. If your mediator actually tries to reason with you, either yell or cry. This will fulfill your obligation to the court, and you won't have to walk out of the negotiation feeling like you were hit by a bus. Following is a story of how you can be duped in mediation:

This particular mediator came very highly recommended. Her very own attorney threw her under the bus by telling her to go to

was Ha-Ha. I win, and you are officially the qua-qua. Just remember when it seems all is lost, it isn't too late to turn the tables.

The moral to the story is: "Never trust a mediator." They do not have your best interest in mind and if your ex is crazier or scarier than you, you'll lose.

CHAPTER 6

Children

IF THERE ARE CHILDREN INVOLVED IN YOUR DIVORCE, REMEMBER THEY ARE THE ultimate victims of this time in their lives. They are losing a parent. Children are not pawns; do not use them as such. If you love your kids, you will not intentionally emotionally scar them. Bad mouthing your ex in front of your children is an ego boost for you, but hurts them in ways that are unimaginable. Be a parent and protect your child. If you don't, then who will?

Every once in a while, a total piece of shit gossip hound may approach you asking what you think of your ex in front of your child. We have found that the best way to deal with this is to give this person, who has nothing better to do than throw shit at the fan, the dirtiest look you can muster and inform them that you think your ex is the person your child loves! LEAVE YOUR KIDS OUT OF THE DEMISE OF YOUR RELATIONSHIP!

We know it sucks when you buy a whole kitchen full of new appliances and then the bitch or bastard kicks you out, but do you really need the appliances? Nope. It may be fun to be pissed off about it, but it won't kill you to walk away from them. Stuff is just stuff and you can always get more.

Keep in mind that you do need important things like your children's well being. Fight about that. Don't torture your kids because you two couldn't work it out. It's not their fault, and no matter how bad it gets between you and the ex, you two will always be their parents. It's not fair for them to have to choose. The better you handle the indignities of divorce, the more your kids will love and appreciate you for it. Ten years from now the only thing they'll remember is who the safe parent was. Make sure you are the safe parent. Don't ever punish your spouse by taking the kids away or poisoning their minds against the ex. It will make you look like the bad one because you are. Besides, your kids can be a wealth of information for you.

There is nothing wrong with picking the kids' brains to get information. You can even plant information to be passed on. The cool thing about kids is that no matter what, they will dime you out. So if there is something you want your ex to know, mention it to the kids and rest assured your ex will find out about it 2 seconds after he picks them up. Casually mention how well you're doing at work and you could be up for that really big promotion.

However, don't forget that this is a double-edged sword. Don't mention promotion unless you expect to pay more child support. It's not a bad idea to keep who you date top secret as this can lead to unfortunate complications, unless you're using your imaginary friend as the bait. This is a great diversion because no one will get hurt, and it will drive your ex nuts trying to figure it out. If your kids report to your ex that you just bought a 60-inch plasma television and you're behind on your child support, this is also a bad thing. Just remember to keep your cards close to your chest. Keeping your kids in the clear needs to be the number one priority.

Always remember that your child is losing a parent and a family unit which is painful enough on its own. Don't add to it by being a jerk.

An exception to this rule is if your ex is dangerous or abusive and you or your child is in danger (be very honest about this). It is your moral obligation to keep everyone safe. You might leave the state. But don't ever dump your emotional issues about your ex on your child under any circumstances.

How to Handle Yourself

You have decided to get rid of that person (even if he filed for divorce first; take control of yourself and make it your decision; it will be much easier for you this way. So what if they beat you to an attorney?). You are brooming the very person who you promised to share your entire life with. The one you promised to love, cherish, and honor. You remember the one who was standing beside you before all your friends and family? You do remember, right? There was probably a church or perhaps a judge, a time when someone said to you "I now pronounce you man and wife till DEATH do you part."

Before you make any rash decisions about arranging the death vow, you need to ask yourself why you want a divorce. Remember the three deal breakers in a relationship: abuse, adultery, or addiction. If you are leaving your ex for any reason other than the ones mentioned, then you are a piece of shit. Who do you think you are? You made these promises that you had no intentions of keeping, or worse yet, maybe you did intend to keep them, but you not only lied to your spouse, but to yourself as well.

If that is the case, the authors of this book hope you develop gangrene in your sexual organs and die a terribly painful death. If you do not die a horrible death and still decide to go through with this divorce, bringing emotional harm to everyone you claim to care about and love, then at least have the common decency to take yourself off the dating market. You have screwed up this relationship; don't go off and start another one. Hurting people because you are psychologically damaged is selfish and you are destroying a perfectly good spouse that someone else could truly love. You are not worthy of love. Give this book to your ex so he can deal with you appropriately.

Other than the Ha-Ha ex and the Qua-Qua ex, there are two other categories that people who are going through divorce fall into. There are the dumpers and there are the dumpees. This is the very beginning of the game. It is important to get the upper hand as soon as possible, but if you missed the boat and your spouse dumped you before you could dump him, it is ok; the game is not over—yet!

CHAPTER 7

Identifying Your Ex

By Mental Illness

We figured that one of the most effective ways to decimate your ex is to identify his weaknesses and use the information to exploit him mercilessly. Christians ask themselves, "What would Jesus do?" We, on the other hand, will be asking, "What would Maslow do?"

We have taken the time to put together a little quiz. This will shed some light on your circumstances and, hopefully, give you the insight to actually apply your own situation to our theory. We hope you will take the time to participate. It's just a simple way to help you know which mental illness you are facing. This allows you to effectively deal with your ex, so you can hit him where it hurts the most. Grab a pencil and be very honest with yourself, then total the points and locate your ex on the list that follows.

1. What does your ex aspire to be when he grows up?
   a) a mermaid
   b) teacher, fireman, or nurse
   c) car salesman or insurance agent
   d) lawyer or cop
2. What is your ex's favorite television show?
   a) The Rock of Love with Brett Michaels on VH1
   b) My Name is Earl

   c) Law and Order
   d) Forensic Files, Snapped, or Murder by the Book on Court TV

3. What was the last book your ex re-read?
   a) Chances by Jackie Collins
   b) The Stand by Stephen King
   c) The Davinci Code by Dan Brown
   d) Getting to Know and Love Jack the Ripper, The Real Man, or any other true crime books that read like a how-to manual.

4. Who is your ex's favorite celebrity?
   a) Jay Leno
   b) Eric Cartman
   c) Susan Sarandon
   d) O.J. Simpson

5. What did your ex get you for the last Valentine's Day when he still liked you?
   a) Dinner, flowers, and something shiny
   b) How to give better head sex manual
   c) Breath mints and a treadmill
   d) A cheap rice steamer and the "I don't love you, never did love you" speech right before he fucked your sister in your bed while you listened.

6. The first time your lying ex said he loved you was:
   a) After nine cocktails
   b) The day he lost his job
   c) The day you won the lottery
   d) He never did

7. What does your ex's favorite sex fantasy involve?
   a) Candles, chocolate, and bubble baths
   b) Having you refer to him by his/your parent's name
   c) Your ass
   d) A donkey

8. Why did your vile ex marry you in the first place?
   a) You were really drunk in Vegas and it sounded like a good idea

b) Someone was knocked up
c) Because the universe or the voices inside his head told him to
d) Because he didn't want you to be able to testify against him in case the Grand Jury actually got that indictment

9. When you suffered a death in your family, or lost a friend, what was the first thing your ex said to you?
   a) What should I wear to the funeral?
   b) That sucks, what did you make for dinner?
   c) Nothing, he just got hysterical so you could take care of him.
   d) What do I get? When is the reading of the will?

10. When you began your divorce proceedings, where did your papers originate?
    a) You went and picked the papers up at the attorney's office to avoid embarrassing process servers
    b) At home in the evening in order to maintain your privacy
    c) At your office
    d) At your birthday party

For every answer that you chose an A, give yourself 5 points, B's are worth 10 points, C's are worth 15 points, and D's are worth 20 points.

If you scored 50 to 100 points, you are dealing with one of the following: An Artist, a Knight in Shining Armor, a Martyr, or a Stoopid.

If you scored 101 to 150 points, you are dealing with one of the following: Philosophers, Obsessive Compulsive Disorder, Liberals, or Manic Depressive.

If you scored 151 points to 200 points, you are dealing with one of the following: A Bipolar, Narcissistic personality disorder, a Socio-path, or a Psychopath.

Now, locate your ex on the list and read up; we're getting to the good stuff.

The following is just a listing of the most common mental afflictions. Please stay objective and do not label your ex with more than one or two titles, as the more specific you can be, the more effective your revenge will be in the long run.

Artists

Yikes, what in the hell were you thinking? Let him go and find himself while you keep all the stuff. Maybe that's what you were thinking. Good call. Seriously, this should be a certified mental disorder. These folks tend to be childish and selfish with a pretty loose grip on reality. They lean toward an emotional train of
thought rather than a logical or rational approach to anything. This is good news for you. All you have to do when dealing with these people is listen intently and reiterate what they just said, changing a few words here and there. They will think you are psychic. They babble and snivel so incessantly they don't even hear themselves most of the time. Use this to your advantage as they are pretty confident that the rest of the human race is as confused as they are. As soon as you have them convinced of your superior slot in their universe, it is time to make some suggestions as to other paths they may choose to follow. If you get really good at this particular mind fuck, you should have your ex growing organic vegetables on a compound in Northern Idaho before the papers are final. Good job! Congratulations, your pension is safe. Don't forget to scare him with the thought of higher powers and karma. He will actually buy that crap. Try a totem of some sort and convince him that this frog or rabbit is "his" animal and any time he needs an answer, or if he is confused about anything, he should focus intently for at least an hour at a time and the answer he seeks will be revealed to him by

the great whatever you came up with. Remember, this is divorce; the gloves are off.

What would Maslow do?

These people like to think of themselves as creative and brilliant. They are the center of their universe. To attack them effectively, Maslow would recommend belittling all of their endeavors and educate them on the fact that the world does not like them. He would not bother to point out their faults. Instead, he would inform them that others perceive them as being worthless and with no talent.

Knights in Shining Armor

If you are fortunate enough to be able to divorce one of these chumps, count your lucky stars. They are pretty much Catholics on steroids. They respond beautifully to whining, crying, and any other demeaning crap you can devise. You can pretty much get anything you want or think you need from these pathetic jellyfish. Swallow your pride and come up with a whopper of a sob story. These people actually take pride in helping someone they perceive as weaker than they. They base their whole sense of self on doing things for other people. When you no longer need them for anything, they will completely lose their identity. They will seek professional counseling while you spend their money on whatever you want. The good news with these guys is that they hardly ever bounce back because they just don't know how to go on unless someone is there to "appreciate" (i.e., take advantage of) all their blood, sweat, and tears. Unless your community has more than its fair share of opportunists, they will mourn until someone else comes along to use them as mercilessly as you just did. That will buy you plenty of time to begin your new life away from "prince/princess charming." You should be long gone with more than your fair share of the marital estate.

What would Maslow do?

These people will climb up the chart on their own, unless someone needs them. They will sacrifice all and sometimes even the first level of Maslow's chart just so they can look themselves in the mirror and say they are good persons. Maslow would cater to their self-righteous practice of being pathetic! He would introduce them to any pathetic down-on-their-luck chump he could find, so that everyone will be happy.

Martyrs

Once again thank your lucky stars. They will do anything you ask; in fact, they will even go one step farther than even you would ever expect. These folks find their identity in whining and bitching to anyone unfortunate enough to be in their vicinity. The worse you screw them over, the happier they are. Just ignore the pity party and laugh all the way to the bank. They thrive on making you look bad no matter what the cost to themselves personally. You need to take the stance  that if you're going to be publicly crucified, you might as well be rewarded monetarily. The bigger bitch or bastard you are to these people, the more they will love to hate you. Hey, everyone wins. They love to be called names and if you can stoke their paranoia with your spies, they will have a great time being the victim. It usually takes these guys years to get over you, and they will spend the rest of their lives reminiscing how bad they got fucked over. You'll be an urban legend and they still won't shut up. Be sure and send them a thank-you note; that will really set them off. Ha-Ha.

What would Maslow do?

Nothing, these people will sink their own boat! He would torture them with converted spies or flat out tell them how he is going to fuck them over. It will all work out as long as everything you tell them is a LIE!

Stoopids

These are the people who insist on making one bad decision after the other. You can feel sorry for them all you want; however, there is no "fix" for these folks as they insist on screwing up so consistently, it is almost comical to watch. It doesn't make you a bad person to enjoy your glee as you watch them mess up over and over, as they were probably cute and good in bed. Once again, thank your lucky
stars, as these folks are benign and after the hurt fades, they can be pretty fun to fuck with. In fact, fucking with these people can become addictive. Too bad they do not have a support group for those of us who are addicted to fucking with the stoopids! It's always a good idea to begin with a good self-esteem bashing. They aren't bright enough to figure out what you are doing. Pick on something they are sensitive about: big ears, crooked nose, pretty much anything will do. Because these people are so dumb, you may try to get them feeling low about something that is imaginary. If they have nice hair, convince

them that it is nappy or, better yet, hit their lack of prowess in the bedroom. Once you knock them off kilter with your snide insults, you can explain options to them. They are incredibly easy to lead and manipulate. It might feel like you're kicking the dog, but they'll still come back and lick your hand, so why stop? You can baffle them with big words and numbers. Throw three things at them at once and you can be confident that they will usually pick the middle option pretty consistently. Make them feel smart by complimenting them when they do what you want, and they'll do it pretty much all the time. Easy enough, you win. Ha-Ha.

What would Maslow do?

Nothing but laugh! He may present them with some decisions that are so simple that a kindergartner would know the right thing to do. When they make the wrong decision time and time again, thereby ruining their lives forever, he would simply chuckle with glee. Hopefully, their parents have a big basement. Ha-Ha.

Philosophers

Once again, what in the hell were you thinking? These people are way above us and while they are in their happy place, you should go ahead and take all their shit. After all, they are not interested in material belongings, so therefore they don't need any. These people are the best to deal with because when confronted with reality and logic they are unsure how to proceed, leaving ample opportunity for you to take  everything. Confuse them with reality as they don't really understand it. While they are busy pondering how exactly you came up with this revelation, you have plenty of time to clean out the bank accounts (don't forget the stock account). Take advantage of their need to over-analyze everything and hit them while they're not looking. By the time they figure out what has happened, you will be long gone. Ha-Ha.

What would Maslow do?

Maslow would verbally compare them to a stoopid and patiently explain why the stoopid is better than they are. He knows anything relating to reason or logic will stupefy them to the point of being unable to function.

OCDs (Obsessive Compulsive Disorders)

These people count everything obsessively and are quite entertaining when intoxicated. They are most effectively dealt with by bombarding them with paperwork full of pointless questions that will take an inordinate amount of time to answer. These are some of the easiest people to deal with as all they require is busy work. Example:

When you are pissed, simply ask how many tiles are in the rest room. That will remove them from your presence and give the cab plenty of time to get there. Hell, you might even meet someone else while waiting. I did. BONUS! Really, all you have to do is set them up. Anything that really doesn't matter to you is your best bet. Get them to focus on that and then while they are figuring out the fundamentals of how many forks and spoons you actually deserve, they will forget about the equity in the house and your investments. That leaves you the time and space you need to deceive them out of the big picture. They will step over a dollar to pick up a penny and so you just need to lay them a copper-colored path to Qua-Quaville.

What would Maslow do?

We have no idea of what Maslow would do, but we know that we cannot seem to stop messing with these good folks; we may go to the special hell, but these people are too much fun!

Liberals

These creatures defy nature. They are so contradictory to themselves it's like trying to reason with a two year-old that is suffering from attention-deficit disorder. They are pretty sure they deserve a free ride but aren't really sure who should pay for it. Then they are pretty sure it should be you because you might be able to afford it, and if you can't, they know they can depend on you to find a way. However, you are the asshole who failed to give them the emotional support they so desperately craved, so they were driven to max your Visa while dating other people. (Why is dating so expensive?) Just understand that everything is your fault when dealing with these people. If you work two jobs to support their habits and lifestyle, it won't be good enough because you won't be there to support their neurosis. Then they'll have an affair and blame it on you because you weren't "there" for them. If you are "there" for them, they won't be happy because you won't be able to afford a new car for them every 6 months. Just understand you can't win for losing with these folks. They'll demand to "know" you at 3 a.m., the whole time knowing damn good and well you have a huge presentation at work due at 8:30 a.m.

The best way to deal with these assholes is to take them to task. Back them into a logical corner making sure there is no way they will be able to weasel out of it. Black and white reasoning is the only way you can trip them up. Once again, they are highly emotional and immune to reason and logic. They figure rules don't apply to them because they don't "feel" that it would be fair to them. When you can corner them and apply the rules to them, they'll get angry. All they will be able to do is call you names and bawl. It's actually very liberating for you at this point because all the bullshit they've been feeding you won't apply at this juncture. It will give you reassurance that you aren't the crazy one. Ha-Ha.

What would Maslow do?

Maslow would attack these people on the most fundamental level. He would try to rob them of shelter and security. He would explain to them that he does not know who should give them a free ride but this bus has stopped! Ha-Ha!

Manic Depressives

This is just a fancy name for being an asshole. However, this isn't as bad as its counterpart (bi-polar disease) as manic depressives are usually more intent on inflicting pain on themselves rather than on other people, which is good news for you. You should be able to have them on suicide watch at the local nut hut with minimal effort. Just repeat over and over the worst  insult you can think of. When they are in the manic state, they will not sleep and will get crazier and crazier the more sleep-deprived they get. Serve them coffee or suggest several big lines of cocaine. It can be exhausting, but well worth it just to get them on video. They will contort their faces and put on quite a show. Keep these home movies to show the judge when they drag you into court seeking a restraining order. You don't need to say a word. Just sit back and observe and admire. They do it to themselves. They will usually come up with some pretty amusing catchphrases all by themselves. Unfortunately for you, they like to have an audience, so if you have to humor them make sure you get something out of it as well. If you are unable to capture them on video, we highly recommend a pocket audio recorder so at least you can play it for the judge. Don't let these people victimize you by playing the victim. Slap them down with a cold hard dose of reality, and they won't have any idea how to respond. Then you can really send them over the deep end.

What would Maslow do?

He would destroy their social standing in the community, which is easily accomplished because everyone already hates them. Just laugh at them in front of their peer group, point out their inconsistencies to everyone they know, and the psycho will take care of the rest on his own. He will usually ostracize himself inside of a month. His only recourse at this time is a new zip code. Yea!!

Bi-Polars

Where do we start? These people are incredibly predictable. One minute they are up, the other they are not. It is rumored that this condition can be treated with medication; we, however, have decided this is just another excuse to be an asshole. These people need

to be watched as they tend to blame everything on you. Unlike a Manic, they tend to want to hurt other people. This is unfortunate for you. They are by no means homicidal (at least not very often, anyway). Just be sure to keep sharp gadgets out of their reach when you are trying to talk to them. It's a good idea to walk on eggshells with these guys because it's impossible to tell what exactly is going to set them off. Communication is best avoided (as much as possible). If you are summoned to sit down with them, bring a witness and a video recorder, with no exceptions. They can be so dangerous you need to keep your safety as a number one priority. Even if you don't suffer physical abuse, they are not above pressing charges on you for an imagined offense. They are very convincing liars and can stay in character for months on end. Well, they got you to marry them right? Be very careful with these folks. Make sure your bases are covered; eventually they will get bored and find someone else who will respond to their demands for drama. Your best bet when dividing your assets with these idiots is to just go ahead and have them committed and take everything while they enjoy a hiatus in the rubber room. Possession is 9/10's of the law so you'll be in good shape when they finally get out. Hopefully, they'll still be highly medicated and won't give a shit anyway.

What would Maslow do?

He would wait until they had a really good day and take it away from them. He would accomplish this by keeping them in the dark on what is really going on until he found them in a good mood, and then he would hit them with everything at once. Keeping them deflated and down, once suicidal impulses take control he would call the funny farm. Then he would start packing.

Narcissistic Personality Disorders

All this requires is a mirror. They aren't very bright and just need to be distracted. In fact, these people don't even deserve to be mentioned. However, if we didn't mention them we would be doing you a disservice. We have had one-on-one experience with this particular animal. Yikes! These

people were born without the part of their brain that produces empathy. In laymen's terms, that means that you mean no more to them than the couch. It is impossible for them to see other people as people. They feel as if they are the most important person on the planet and the rest of us are here strictly for their amusement and entertainment. They will suffer psychotic episodes from time to time, and then it is important for you to call the funny farm. They also suffer from sleep deprivation and, we can tell you from experience, if they can't sleep, neither will anyone else. They will make demands on you that will take your breath away. You can rest assured that they have been planning your assassination since the wedding ceremony, so please don't lose a wink of sleep over fucking these assholes over as hard as you can. Unlike Sociopaths and Psychopaths, they aren't very smart; they just think they are. That is a huge bonus for you. As usual, with any mentally ill individual, a good dose of reality will set them on their ass. While they are screaming and demanding explanations, the most effective way to send them over the moon is to smile serenely and say Ha-Ha. Don't ever let these people rile you because they thrive on that control. The more neutral you are toward them, the crazier they will get. If you refuse to stroke their ego, they can't maintain control of themselves, which is exactly where you want them. They might break some stuff but are too full of themselves to actually risk incarceration. Understand that in their reality, jail is way beneath them; remember the rules don't apply to them. If you can get them thrown in the clink, it is the ultimate insult and while they are serving their sentence, you can take all the stuff. It wouldn't be a bad idea to leave town if it's not too big of a hassle. Otherwise, it's a pretty safe bet that they will leave the state to go on to a smaller pond where they can be the big fish. The best analogy we can come up with for this particular class of people is that they are truly King or Queen shit of turd mountain and that's where they belong. Attack their pride until they lose control and then hit them with the consequences and you shouldn't have any more trouble. Ha-Ha (quietly, you'd hate to rouse the other prisoners).

What would Maslow do?

He would take away their ability to control even themselves, pointing out all along the way how low in the dung heap these people actually reside. In the grand scheme of things these guys don't amount to shit.

Sociopaths

Uh-Oh. These people are down-right dangerous. The American prison system is overrun with these folks. Ninety percent of violent criminals suffer from this particular personality disorder. The best advice you can heed when dealing with these guys is to either move out of the country using a false identity, or never show fear, then have someone plant enough illegal narcotics on them to send them away for a long, long time.

You'll actually be doing them and society a favor. These people thrive in our penal system. These are the guys you read about in the paper that get a lighter sentence because the homicide was committed in "the heat of passion." Uh Oh, no matter what frame of mind it was committed in, you're still dead! Never show fear with these people because they perceive it as weakness. The only way to walk out of a tough spot with these guys is to convince them that you are crazier than they are and you have more friends with felony convictions. Terrorist activity is what these assholes thrive on and the only thing they understand is violence and hatred. If they detect any kind of weakness in you, forget it, you're dead. Keep this in mind when you want to cry and plead; your very survival depends on your ability to back that asshole down. It can be done. Then get the hell out of there and run to somewhere safe. The police aren't really an option because they never take you seriously in time. Start hanging out at the local biker bar and pretend you know the people they're talking about. It's pretty effective and with any luck the bikers are a little less crazy than your ex. Look at the bright side: The common sociopath is driven by emotion and won't stop to apply logic, so if you are able to work them into a frenzy in a "safe" environment, they will be sure to do something rash and stupid and you will have plenty of time to change your name, then get the hell out of Dodge before they're able to get out on parole.

What would Maslow do?

Move to Connecticut.

Psychopaths

Once again, Uh-Oh. Hope you weren't stupid enough to procreate with this person. Either you need your head examined or there was tequila involved. These people are usually highly intelligent, witty, charming, and won't hesitate to gut you like an animal carcass. They will have no remorse. RUN! We have bad news for you. These people have no emotions and are incapable of remorse. When they have you in their cross hairs, it is

strictly business. Everything they inflict on you is methodical and planned so thoroughly you will never even see it coming. Remember the Chinese fortune cookies that say "still waters run deep?" They were probably thinking of a psychopath. They are highly intelligent and cunning. Think Hannibal Lector in "Silence of the Lambs." You won't read about these people in the newspapers; but your family will read about you in the newspapers because you've gone missing.

It's impossible to work them into an emotional frenzy; however, negotiation isn't out of the question. They will respond to reason and logic. If you give them everything they want and don't piss them off too badly, you might just survive. These assholes will hold a grudge forever, so hopefully they didn't catch you in the sack with anyone else.

Another effective way to deal with these people is to convince them that you are crazier than they are. You must be completely irrational and emotional. IF you can scream louder and produce more fake tears and snot than them, you have a chance at scaring them off. This usually doesn't work with a male psychopath. However, if you are dealing with a female psychopath this just may work. They will figure that it is much better for them to play the victim and will take that role all the way. The victim role got really great reviews and if they have tits, they will usually fare better in the system rather than trying to fuck you out of your measly pension and equity.

Just try and find solace in the fact that if you married one of these wretched people, they couldn't love you. It isn't you, it's just that they lack the capacity to feel any kind of emotion, so just pity them and get on with your life. Hopefully, you won't need to use your organ donor card before you're out.

What would Maslow do?

He would get a new identity and move somewhere warm. He would also take sharpshooter classes and apply for a concealed weapon permit.

These are just general guidelines to follow when making your plan. Divorce is a very intricate game of mental chess. You must never underestimate your opponent. It's kind of disappointing to overestimate them. After all, you were the dumb ass who married them in the first place. But in the long run overestimation is by far the better path to choose. That way there are no nasty surprises waiting to bite you in the ass!

One thing you can take solace in is that no matter what the affliction your ex (or possibly you) suffers from, we are all human. We all need the same basic things. As the ex-spouse you should know best where to take your ex out. Psychology 101 teaches Maslow's chart. Remember? While waging war, it is important to remember Maslow's first tier and use it to your advantage. Because it is a felony to choke the life out of someone else, air is out. What else do you have? Let's think for a minute. It is also a felony to poison someone, so the food and water is out too. That leaves shelter and sex. Short of burning down the hovel they live in (also a felony), that leaves sex.

This brings us to a quagmire of decisions that only you can answer. Can you still have sex with your ex? Some of us can. Is it worth it? That is something that is a personal decision. It's not an option for one of us. We'd much rather commit one or all of the aforementioned felonies than lay down with that piece of shit again. However, there are you stout souls out there who are so cold this isn't a problem for you. Good job. Here are some suggestions on exactly how you can work this in your favor.

CHAPTER 8

Grudge Fucking & the Art of Insult & Revenge

REVENGE IS A DISH BEST SERVED COLD. EVERYONE HAS HEARD IT, BUT WHAT does it really mean? Revenge is a lot of fun, especially if there are no dire consequences. Because you really want to get even, the best approach is to do it subtly. For instance, if your ex insists on pissing all over the seat and the floor when taking a leak, you should feel entitled to revenge. After all, if he is that big of a slob, he's not the one that is cleaning the loo anyway. When cleaning your urine-stained floor and bowl what better tool to use than his toothbrush? That way when he's brushing his teeth, you can smile and have a brighter day. The whole time no one is the wiser and you have something to chuckle about that will last forever. This will also remove any temptation you may have of ever kissing him again so you can safely get drunk in his presence and laugh the whole time. You'll never have to worry about your hormones getting out of control and leading you astray.

Some people never get the idea of revenge: If your ex pisses on your pillow, you should thank your lucky stars that he's gone and seek counseling immediately after hiring a "guy" to take that one out of the gene pool forever. The whole idea of revenge is to make your ex look bad, or harm him in some way that makes you happy, not to lower yourself to something even the dog wouldn't ever do, cats maybe, but never your dog.

You know that your ex is going to tell everyone what you did to him, so don't get caught. It makes it so much easier to smile at him if you're trying not to laugh because you know what you did and he does not have a clue. It also makes the "never let him see you cry" rule much easier to follow. However, if you pissed on his pillow, he is going to know about it and tell everyone he knows and you'll be forever known as that "person" who never finished potty training. You'll never get laid again, and if you do, good God, by whom? You'll never live something like that down; it's unbelievably sick and twisted without even a morsel of Ha-Ha. It's just not worth it; exercise some class and think things through before you take action.

It is important to keep this in perspective. Grudge fucking is cruel, evil, and one step above rape whether it is done to a male or a female. This method of humiliation will not be endorsed by either one of the authors of this book, but if it is one of the methods that you are heartless enough to employ, you'll probably win. You need to realize that grudge fucking is an art. It is important to catch your ex in a moment of weakness. You need to identify him in his most vulnerable state and then pounce. Remember you are the cat and he is the mouse. This can be one of your most deadly weapons. Most important, you must make him understand immediately afterward that you have knocked him down another notch. Following is a list of comments that are highly recommended to use immediately post-sex. Just beware: After dropping one of these little gems, you'll never see the inside of that bedroom again, ever.

Post Coital Comments

It's not you ... Yes, it is.

Ha-Ha.

Hey that was really great, your best ever actually, but I'm really tired of treating you like shit. There is not a logical argument for this one. YIKES!

Thanks, Babe, but you're still not it; I'm looking for that one really SPECIAL person.

Oh yeah, that's why I left! Bye.

I have a date in 15 minutes, do you mind seeing yourself out?

Oh, by the way, you need to call public health, my test was positive.

I never noticed how big your (fill in the blank i.e. ears, ass, etc., [not dick or tits] is).

When they utter the dreaded "I love you" phrase deep in the night, simply pat them on the head and call them your drunken buddy.

Don't call ... ever.

Videotape the encounter and use it for blackmail later.

You know it is a good thing you do not try to make a living doing this. You'd starve to death!

If you don't have the stomach to say any of these things out loud (it takes cement balls), there are other ways to get your point across. You can always find a friend with crabs, put some in a jar and leave a deposit. Pat them on the head and leave. Or a nice note or poem will do. Try something like Roses are red, Violets are blue, I have herpes and so do you, bitch/bastard.

However you do it, make sure you are the first to walk, and walk away quickly. This form of revenge is particularly cold-hearted, but extremely effective. It is usually best used by men, as guys are gifted with the ability to fuck someone and walk away totally unscathed. Women, on the other hand, are cursed with that whole nesting estrogen bullshit. This one can be dangerous, so just make sure you're doing this with the proper motives.

If fucking your ex is too nauseating for words, another option is to fuck someone who is close to your ex: a sibling, or a best friend; hell, even a parent is a possibility. As long as you're sure your ex finds out as soon as possible.

There are all sorts of ways to demean your ex while waging war. Our goal here is to add a bit of a creative twist. While name calling is typically low class and not recommended, sometimes it becomes necessary. It's best if you practice beforehand and come to the table armed with creative alternatives to the typical stuff. "Fucking bitch" isn't that big of a deal. If you can come with an arsenal of colorful explicatives, that will usually shut 'em up. Following is a list of pre-approved "this conversation is over" phrases guaranteed to get you out of the room.

1. Two pump chump.

2. You're fat and you smell bad.

3. I'm bored and tired of treating you like shit.

4. You need to shut your whore face up before I have to come over there and fuck-start your head.

5. Don't stand on my dick or I'll have to put one in ya.

6. How about I cut a hole in ya and drink a cocktail while I watch ya bleed out.

7. Do you know how I know you're gay? Fill in the blank: i.e., you drive a corvette. But not for much longer. Ha-Ha.

8. I may have been in a blackout then, and I may be in a blackout now.

9. Explain to them that you would rather throw a sideways fuck into a rancid cat than to lay down with them again, ever.

10. Viagra boy.

11. Dirty Hippie (take your patchily stink and hit the bricks!).

12. Captain fruit boots.

13. Goat boy.

14. Toot.

15. Fuckwitt.

16. Fart ass.

17. Fucktard.

18. If you had as many dicks sticking out of you as you have had stuck in you ... You would look like a God-Damn porcupine ... Whore.

19. You're a big piece of after-birth.

This is guaranteed to get you out of a sticky situation and stop all conversation immediately. It is also a good idea to practice these if you are dealing with a psychopath and need to throw a temper tantrum. Always go prepared.

CHAPTER 9

Identifying Your Ex Through Astrology

Iғ ʏᴏᴜʀ ᴇx ᴅᴏᴇsɴ'ᴛ sᴜꜰꜰᴇʀ ꜰʀᴏᴍ ᴏɴᴇ ᴏꜰ ᴛʜᴇ ᴀꜰᴏʀᴇᴍᴇɴᴛɪᴏɴᴇᴅ ᴍᴇɴᴛᴀʟ illnesses, you can always turn to astrology. As much as we would like to downplay and negate this form of diagnosis, keep in mind that this is a 2000-year-old tradition and there's got to be something to it. The Chinese didn't go to all that trouble charting stuff to be completely negated by western science. There is a reason "hey baby, what's your sign?" was the hottest pick-up line in the seventies. If you married out of your element, that will explain everything.

For those of you who have no idea what we're talking about, there are four elements in nature: Earth, Fire, Water, and Air. If you foolishly mismatched your elements, you are, as we speak, feeling the sting of bad karma. You should know your ex's birthday and his sign. You should have checked this long before you made the death march down the aisle that led straight to Hell. For instance, Air and Fire are wonderful together; in fact, you can't have Fire without Air. However, we all know what happens when you mix Fire and Water. Water wins, usually, unless there's not enough of it. Hey, we all love a good sauna. It all depends on the individual sign. Julie is a Leo; she accidentally got knocked up by a Cancer. Fire and Water (God-damn that tequila). Needless to say, it didn't work out so well or she wouldn't be writing this book. She is ashamed to say that was her first divorce. She didn't like being out in the rain. The second divorce was from a Gemini. A sort of better match, as Gemini is an Air sign; unfortunately he suffered from narcissistic personality disorder. He was certified and had been committed for that particular disorder several times. That would've been really handy information to have before her drunken stagger down the aisle. Too bad he had an average sized head. His mother actually dropped that little bombshell during his first psychotic episode she had the misfortune to witness. Keep in mind that astrology is only to be relied on when your ex doesn't suffer from one of those pesky mental illnesses. Please locate your ex's sign in the following list as we have devised a way to find his fundamental weaknesses and how to use it against him, mercilessly.

Just a note: If you fuck up on your paperwork, blame it on the fact that Mercury was in retrograde. No one can argue with the universe.

The four elements and their corresponding signs:

Fire: Leo, Sagittarius, Aries (compatible with Air and other fire signs).

Water: Cancer, Pisces, Scorpio (Compatible with Earth and other water signs).

Earth: Taurus, Capricorn, Virgo (Compatible with other Earth signs, no one else likes them).

Air: Gemini, Aquarius, Libra (Compatible with Fire, that's it, these guys don't even like themselves).

Once you have located yourself and your ex on the above list, you can tell if you married outside your element. If you did, you can always blame the planets because it's no longer fun to place the blame squarely on your ex. Another good place to lay blame is on the tides, weather, new lovers, or the dog. We never want to run out of scapegoats. After all, we're sure you were the perfect spouse and never did anything wrong. We're strong proponents of denial. It's lovely there in the spring. If you're stubborn enough, you can stay there for a lifetime. Good luck.

Capricorn

The sign of the Goat—This explains that earthy aroma that surrounds you when your ex is in the room. Please feel free to explain to these people that they do indeed smell like a goat, and that is why you will never have sex with them again ever. If you have the pleasure of divorcing one of these folks, be aware that they have the tendency to become selfish and ruthless. On the positive side, they suffer from loneliness and depression; you can use this against them. Simply point out every time you speak to them that no one likes them and they are certain to be alone forever. Maybe you should buy them a kitten and explain that they should appreciate a box of shit in the house as this will mask their own earthy aroma. HA-HA.

These people will most likely suffer from manic depression, if you are fortunate enough to get one that is certifiable. Keep in mind if you play your cards right these guys can be driven to suicide with minimal effort.

Aquarius

The sign of the Water Bearer—The majority of these folks are indeed certifiable. They suffer mostly from Artist Syndrome. They are not in touch with reality as the rest of us understand it. Reasoning with these people is like trying to explain quantum physics to Billy Bob, your local gas station attendant. Good luck with that.

When you do battle with these folks, it is important to keep in mind that they will detach and become very absentminded (yea!). They also exhibit paranoia and neurosis (even better!). They will refuse to cooperate and, if you're lucky, they'll hide behind their lawyer so you can cost them an obscene amount of money. Use their eccentric behavior against them. It doesn't really do any good to videotape these guys because they are consistently crazy and never visit the land of Ha-Ha where the rest of us live. On second thought, maybe you should record them, as judges tend to appreciate those things. You can screw with these people for days and weeks, but it's not very fun as they don't really care about your retirement or investments. Most of them don't mind living in a shack. So, congratulations; even if you did marry outside of your element, you picked a patsy. Well done. Ha-Ha.

Pisces

The sign of the Fish. Flush that bastard. These people will most likely suffer from obsessive compulsive disorder. They are weak, weak beings. This is great news for you. They are timid, they lie, they lean a lot toward lazy, and they will slip into masochism. This is fantastic news for the future ex-to-be. Break their will, honestly, how hard can it be? Your

divorce attorney will thank you for it. You can strip these people of their very being if you handle them accordingly. Explain to them that they were the worst piece of ass you ever had the misfortune of having, and the only reason you married them was out of pity. Get them fired and give them a bag of pot for their birthday. Encourage their slothfulness so you can pounce on them when they are down. After you have completely destroyed any chance at a future these puss bags may have once had, you can usually encourage them to enter into the adult entertainment industry as a restroom attendant. Ha-Ha.

Aries

The sign of the Ram—Ever won-der why we refer to "it" as horny? If you have ever studied the package of Trojan condom wrappers you'll notice that a large part of their logo depicts the ram. There is a good reason for that. These people are of the first sign of the zodiac, so they do come by their infantile

personalities honestly. They are completely self-absorbed and unable to concentrate on anything other than themselves. They are the cul-mination of all the mental illnesses. They are incapable of monogamy or anything else that resembles the "decent" thing to do. Even if they are totally wrong about everything, you will never be able to concern them with anything that doesn't involve them directly. The best way to handle these idiots is to dangle something shiny in front of them and distract them. Let them think they have something that you re-ally, really want. As long as they have the illusion of control, you'll be able to do whatever you want.

Taurus

The Bull—Count your lucky stars. Taurus people are typically the biggest martyrs on the planet, and this can be extremely helpful when manipulating them into doing whatever you want. These people

are incredibly obstinate and exhibit an exhilarating lack of reason. As long as you disagree with them you win. No matter what it may be about, big issues versus small doesn't matter to them. These guys are the ultimate mind fucks. They will do whatever it takes to "ruin" you, even if it's to their detriment. They are so short-sighted and bad at reasoning you've got it made. Just look at them with wide eyes and say "Oh my God, I'd hate to be stuck in that house, it's way too much to vacuum." They will, in turn, insist you keep the house just because it gives them something to feel sorry for themselves about. They'll tell everyone how evil and horrible you are so you might as well make them happy and be a bastard. Then laugh all the way to the bank. You can't win with these people as they have a canny knack at making you the bad guy. Doesn't matter what you do, you're wrong, so it's best not to let them down. Whatever you want, ask for the opposite and your ignorant Taurus will shove everything you asked for right down your throat, just to teach you a lesson. Keep in mind these guys are only happy when they're miserable, so it's best to accommodate them.

Gemini

The sign of the Twins—Let me tell ya, these are some pretty weird cats. They suffer from schizophrenia and acquired narcissistic personality disorders. They get two mental illnesses because there are, in fact, two of them. This sucks, because you never know who's home when they answer the  phone. Some of them have a good side and a bad side. Most of them have two horrible sides and one just wears a smiley face mask. Watch out for these guys. One side will tell you that you are wonderful and could they please have $20.00 while the "other one" is screwing your sister. They lean toward shallowness, unreliability, and self-deception. If you can help these guys delude themselves into the nut hut, you win. Ha-Ha.

Cancer

The Crab—We hope you didn't catch a case of the crabs from this one. These people are incapable of loyalty or honor. They are insidious and just like their name, Cancer, they tend to resemble large ugly tumors with a spiky shell. They are moody, stingy, irritable, clingy, and worst of all, cowardly. They can be dangerous, but not to your face;

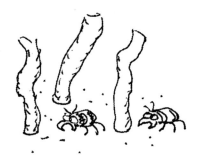

they're too chickenshit for that. They best way to handle these folks is from afar. Poke them with a really long stick and run them around in circles. Needless to say, these folks have psychosis as their mental illness. The only glitch you're going to run into is that they will get homicidal instead of suicidal which is unfortunate for you. If you're divorcing one of these folks, we will extend our condolences now and suggest you go get yourself a new hatchet. Best of luck and remember to keep your distance. Don't forget to check your brakes.

Leo

The Lion—Ignore the name, these folks are fairly benign. They are arrogant and suffer horribly from pride, which is always good to use against people. Watch out when they quit roaring as they tend to scratch. The most common mental ailment that these folks suffer from is "Knight In Shining Armor." Your Leo will love to rescue you. If you act pathetic enough, they'll rescue

themselves right into the poorhouse. The key is to never yell at them or call them names. These beasts react poorly to that kind of abuse, and you are liable to lose a limb. They are reasonably intelligent but inherently lazy so you'll be able to use that to your advantage as well. Just run them ragged long enough and they'll eventually just give up and go away. Then you say Ha-Ha.

Virgo

The Virgin—These folks tend to like splitting hairs and over-analyzing everything to death. They can be highly critical and cranky. They mostly suffer from being philosophers. As long as they can get on their soap boxes, they're likely to be out of your house, which is good for you. Throw lots of crap and hope enough sticks that while they are moaning and groaning, you can take whatever you want. The more these people can feel kicked around, the happier they are. They tend to be very pessimistic so if you can make them miserable and poor, everyone wins. See how easy that is? Ha-Ha.

Libra

The Scales—Don't let the name fool you. These people are about as out of whack as it gets. They tend to lean toward the liberal side of things and no amount of reasoning with them will give you an edge. They are terrible procrastinators and can't make a decision to save their souls. That works out well for you because you can make the decision for them. Because they will wait until the last minute, make your deadlines as short as possible. With any luck they'll miss most of them and you'll win by default. They are usually guilty of pleasure seeking, so if there is anyway to introduce them to the world of illicit drugs you'll have it made. Keep your fingers crossed for an overdose and keep as much of your stuff as you can. Ha-Ha.

Scorpio

The Scorpion—They are the original sociopath. These folks care nothing about you, their family, or anyone or anything that isn't themselves They are ruthless, sadistic, fanatical, and hell bent on revenge. They don't care who they hurt, and if they can leave a trail of  despair and carcasses behind them, they are in their element. Because they are full of self-loathing, they are suspicious of anything you do. Just listen to them and you can be sure that anything they accuse you of they are indeed guilty of doing it themselves. These folks are evil, evil, evil. You're not going to win with these chumps no matter what you do, so just try to get out with your mind and body intact. Never cross them directly, as they are likely to take a contract out on you. They will lie, cheat, and steal just to make you look bad. The best way to handle these guys is indirectly. Get as far away as you can, then start making things happen in their lives that even the most insane Scorpio will never link back to you. We recommend giving their address to your local chapter of Hell's Angels and telling them that the narc that took down their brother lives there. Good luck and God speed.

Sagittarius

The Archer—These guys are usually the life of the party. They can be reckless, careless, and really rude. You'll find these folks pretty stupid; therefore, handily dealt with. They become confused so easily you can have them questioning their basic foundation. Hell, handled properly you can convince these idiots they're gay. How much fun can you have with one of these clowns? The possibilities are endless. We recommend that you drop to your knees and thank your lucky stars you had the foresight to marry an imbecile. They go away pretty quickly and sadly enough they're pretty easy to forget about altogether. They were fun while it lasted, but you should be able to leave your union to the Archer relatively unscathed. Congratulations and Ha-Ha.

We hope this brief synopsis of astrological signs will give you some ideas of how to handle your particular ex. The more effectively and efficiently you deal with them, the quicker you can start to live again. The whole idea is to make them feel like they've had a frontal lobotomy and to understand beyond a shadow of a doubt that you are superior to them and you are not to be crossed, ever. The worse your nickname is, the better you have done your job. So when the fur starts to fly, you'll know just how to hit below the belt and knock the wind out of your scheming, lying, but, alas, inferior ex. All you have to do is say Ha-Ha.

CHAPTER 10

Methods of Defense

PLAYING THE VICTIM

Dear Trey and Julie,

My ex has painted me as a monster to all of our friends. She is telling them that I am abusive and that I have hit her. She does try to provoke a fight whenever she is in the same room with me. When I try to get away from her, she will physically use her body to back me up against a wall or into a corner to prevent me from escaping her childish temper tantrums. She has told my friends that I am psychologically abusive and that she is concerned for the welfare of our children when they are with me. What can I do?

Monster Man

Dear Monster Man,

Your ex is trying to cut down on your social circle. Keep your head high and take note of the people who fall for her lies; they are not your friends, but they will make awesome spies. The sympathy she is receiving from your "friends" is putting her on cloud nine. Never try to justify yourself to your friends; let your past speak for you. If you start justifying yourself now you will have to justify yourself throughout the rest of your divorce. Instead, ask your friends if they believe her. If they say "yes," then let them know that you accept their low opinion of you. Never speak to that person again, unless you can use them for something. If they say "no," then ask them why you are having this conversation.

Trey (fellow monster) and Julie

There is an art to playing the victim. The goal of being the victim is not to obtain sympathy from your friends and family. Rather, the goal is to acquire court admissible documentation. This documentation can get you the sympathy of the courts if you do have to go before a judge. Playing the victim as a female is easy; pretend you are afraid of your ex. If no one is looking or if the only people in the room are the people you trust, invade his body space until he is backed up against the wall; use your body to prevent them from leaving a room. Yell at him with your nose 2 inches away from his and push as many of his buttons as you can. With a little bit of luck he may push you away then you can send his ass to jail. HA-HA, the stupid jerk should have refused to see you in a face-to- face! Now you can label him as an abusive prick!

It is a little bit more difficult to play the victim as a male. Trey's ex-wife made a beautiful victim during their divorce. She spent quite a bit of her time portraying him as the devil himself. The funny thing about this is that she was the aggressive and dangerous one. It was pretty common for Trey to get threatening phone calls or hear threats through the grapevine. She used all the tactics that were just described for playing the victim as a female. At one time during their divorce her friends took it into their heads to follow him around town. They thought he would take it as a threat. Yea them!!! They guessed right! Trey views the people that his ex-wife took to hanging around with to be unstable. It was fortunate that when he discovered that he was being stalked by his soon-to-be ex-wife's friends, he happened to be at a good friend's house. So they wrote down the license plate number and called the police. Because of the threats and other occurrences that the police had been called about, it was suggested that he seek protection from an organization that helps people with domestic violence. In the city where he lives the only place that is equipped to deal with domestic issues is the women's shelter. Because he is a male, they were unable to let him stay at their facility, but they did put him up in a hotel. But more important, he obtained great documentation. It showed how the ex-wife was using her friends to stalk and harass him. It would have not taken much to get a restraining order against her at that point, but Trey decided to use this as a bargaining chip to obtain things that he wanted. Blackmail is an ugly word, but it sure is useful. We prefer referring to blackmail as immoral honesty.

In the state of Wyoming, if you are trying to get a divorce, both parties have to go through mediation. When he went to his mediation, he explained to the lady who did this service for them that he did not want to be left in the room alone with his ex. The lady frowned at him and said, "She looks pretty harmless to me." He explained what a beautiful victim she played and informed her that he was not afraid of her assaulting him. He was afraid that she was going to walk past him, fall down, and claim that he had tripped her. She was 6 months pregnant with her married lover's baby. He did not want to take a risk of anything she might try. Just as a side note, he takes extreme pleasure knowing that this guy was not only married, but dumped her immediately after learning she was knocked up. HA-HA. Playing the victim is very important, but it is especially important if you are male. Remember, never be within striking distance of the ex because if you are close enough to strike her, then you are close enough for her to say that you struck her.

SPIES

Dear Trey and Julie,

My ex seems to know EVERYTHING that is going on in my life. How is he doing this?! All I want to do is live my life away from him, but he seems to think he needs to know about every little detail of my world. Any suggestions?

Bugged

Dear Bugged,

Your ex has cut down on your sense of security. Before you can effectively turn the tables on your ex, you need to ask yourself "So what?" So what if your ex knows that you have a new lover? So what if your ex knows you got a new job, car, house etc? It does not matter. Let him spend all of his time and effort researching you. It does not matter and only hurts him. Be secure in the knowledge that even though he has this information on you, there is not Jack Shit he can do with it!!

If you have something to hide, you need to put forth the effort to figure out where exactly the information is coming from. Then you can feed the mole information that is totally benign. Keep your financial information close to the cuff and have a good time with the rest.

Good Luck! Trey and Julie

DRAMA, DRAMA, DRAMA! People love drama. Throughout your relationship with your ex, you have been making friends who know and like both you and your ex. These people do not want to be put in the middle of your dispute, but at the same time they want to know what is going on. It is like a train wreck: You do not want to look but you can't help it. Some of these people will feel a loyalty toward you, some of them will feel a loyalty to your ex, and some of them will not feel loyalty for either of you and are able to stay completely neutral. Trey has been divorced from his first ex-wife for 11 years and people still occasionally tell him what is going on in her life. He just listens and then gives them the response that he thinks is appropriate. He has not seen the woman in 11 years; he really doesn't care what she is up to, but at least he gets a nice conversation with his friend. Now can we talk about the weather?

Spies fall into three categories: my spies, their spies, and converted spies. Your friends will be more than happy to tell you what evil vile thing your ex has said or what you are being accused of this week; that is what friends are for, to watch your back. Their spies are

72

the people who come visit you and listen to talk about your feelings and what is going on in your life, then immediately go and tell your ex. Converted spies are created by you.

It may come to your attention that your ex seems to know way too much of what is going on in your life, such as if you are seeing someone, who it is, your schedule, who you are hanging out with, and what your plans are. How is he finding this out? Did he bug your house? Maybe he is stalking you. How the hell does he know this stuff? The answer is simple and pretty mundane. You have a hole in your friend network. Someone you trust is leaking information to your ex. Here is how you figure out who it is. Tell each suspected person a different lie, then wait to see which one comes back to you. It will surprise you where the leak is. My ex was able to learn all kinds of information about me so I told everyone a different lie. My leak turned out to be a co-worker who I didn't even realize was acquainted with my ex. Once you know who your spy is DO NOT CONFRONT THEM!! USE THEM!!

You can pass all kinds of fun information to your ex through a converted spy. For instance, once Trey learned who his spy was, he pulled the spy aside and told him that every once in a while he would go and look for his ex's car, just so he would know where she was spending her nights. The very next day he was accused of searching the town for her car. His ex's friend told him that he did not need to bother searching for her car anymore because his ex was hiding it now. HA-HA. While she was hiding her car, he was at home sleeping soundly. Another time he told his converted spy that his ex left some of her stuff at his house so he had pawned it. She called him up mad as hell and asked him where he had pawned her stuff. He told her that he had no idea what she was talking about! HA-HA. He did not have anything of hers; we bet she went nuts looking for all of her imaginary stuff.

One day Trey's son was sick and was puking all night long. Needless to say when he went to work the next day he was exhausted. When his converted spy asked him why he was so tired, he told him that he spent the night sitting outside of his ex's apartment watching her! Later that day when his ex came to see him, he spoke to her through the window, as he was not dumb enough to be alone with the vile woman. She accused him of stalking her! Can you believe that? She even told him that he had been seen the previous night in his car outside of her apartment. Of course, it was a complete lie. He was at home taking care of their sick child. He laughed in her face and thanked her for letting him know that he needed to hide better. He even suggested that the next time she saw him, she should call the police. Mad as hell she assured him that she would. HA-HA.

Fun Things to Leak to a Converted Spy

1. You are stalking your ex.
2. You think you gave your ex VD.
3. You are going to move away.
4. You have moved on and have a new love interest. If you have the right kind of ex, they will go nuts trying to figure out who it is!
5. You pawned their stuff: DVD's, clothes etc.
6. You suspect your ex cheated on you and you know who with. Tell your spy that the lover admitted to it. If it is true, your ex will be mad at his new lover, and if it is not true, your ex will blame the friend for stirring up shit.
7. That you heard your mother-in-law has cancer. This can be fun. When you approach your spy pretend to be really upset about it.
8. That you're pretty sure your sister-in-law is pregnant by you.
9. The IRS has served them with papers for announcing their audit.
10. There is a warrant for his arrest.
11. He missed court. There is currently a warrant out for his arrest.
12. Anything else you can think of that might annoy your ex. Be sure to give your converted spy bits of truth. You want your ex to believe them for as long as possible!

that jerk. Imagine her dismay when she arrived and the mediator demanded that she be left alone in the room with the very man that she had a restraining order against. Already the fear and stress of seeing the psychopath ex was working against her. We'll refer to her as the Dumb Ass Cash Cow. Why not? He did.

Hindsight is always 20/20 and it is important to know you have the right to leave mediation for any reason. It is kind of like overeating. Know when to walk away from the table; otherwise, you can develop a huge case of heartburn and indigestion that will never go away. Know your rights and don't be afraid to demand them.

The Dumb Ass Cash Cow had finally been pushed into the slaughter house ass first. Imagine her dismay when the mediator and judge not only granted palimony, but they did it in the state of Wyoming, a state that doesn't even recognize alimony. They called it spousal support to make her feel better but it didn't work; she still felt like shit.

The ex wasn't even a cute Liberal Californian. His prowess as a lover wasn't worth a damn and his boobs had grown bigger than hers. She had also just learned of a hobby he neglected to mention, putting small animals in the microwave oven for fun; just sounded sick and wrong, especially when he was leering at her over his man-boob crack. She should have stuck with her dog and bought a good vibrator. It would have saved her a fortune.

Just when the Cash Cow was at her lowest and was in danger of becoming the qua-qua ex, suddenly an idea sprouted. While she was whining incessantly to her loyal and somewhat drunken support system, inspiration struck!

That bastard hadn't been paying his child support to the fine state of California. The Cash Cow (no longer dumb ass) placed a call to the State and gave them the escrow account information where the Liberal Californian's blood money was held. When he showed up to pick up the cash, all he got was a receipt from California.

To make matters even funnier, he had been borrowing marijuana against the money that he was expecting. Needless to say, he had a lot of pissed off people wanting their money. All she had to say

Other Defense Strategies

As fun and valuable as spies are, there are other methods of defense that should be discussed.

1. Make sure that your movements are concealed from your ex. Never gloat to your ex about what you are going to do. They will find out what you have been up to when it happens and it is far too late for them to do anything about it. You may want to avoid mentioning your plans to your friends until after the ex has been damaged by your actions. Keeping your ex guessing is a major form of defense. If he does not know your movements then he cannot prepare for them. This also has a tendency of unnerving him enough to do something foolish like have his friends follow you around town. HA-HA.

2. Keep your ex protecting areas that you have no intention of attacking. If your ex has money, but you feel that the money belongs to him and not to you, tell him that you are going to take it from him, while you are in reality taking something that you feel you do have a right to, but he does not want you to have. Like your DVD collection.

3. If you do not know what your ex may be planning for you in the divorce strategy, it is usually a good idea to goad him into gloating or to threaten you. It is surprising how many people have no real strategies when playing this game. It kind of depends on how aggressive your ex is. This can be ascertained by the level of mental illness that he suffers from. If he suffers from any of the final six then this will work beautifully. If he suffers from the first six he is too stupid and you shouldn't waste your energy.

4. Discredit your ex. Lying to friends and family tends to blow up in your face. Instead, bait a trap for your ex. Provide your ex with an opportunity to make an outlandish accusation publicly. Make sure it can easily be disproved. For example, convince your ex that you are stalking him. Of course, make sure that the time you pick to have been allegedly stalking him would be impossible for

it to be true. This will discredit him with his friends and support group.

5. What is your ex's biggest argument or complaint about you? Is there any way you can publicly remove that complaint? Giving them nothing to bitch about (at least publicly) will steal a lot of their thunder and their justification.

6. Distract your ex with life problems. Forcing small changes to his routine will keep him off balance and will be a nuisance. Give him something else to think about other than you. There are many ways to do this. It may be as simple as putting your child in a daycare that is a pain in the ass for him to visit. Or signing him up for several hundred magazines to disrupt his mail. You could also put in a change of address for him. When your ex develops a love interest it will be a God send. You have very little control over that one, but you may be able to send him potential lovers for rejection. You can tell these potential lovers that your ex once told you how attracted he was to them. It may or may not be true. This will prove to be a great tactic to use because they will keep calling him and chasing him. If you are lucky your ex will start devoting his time and effort into the new relationship, leaving you free to attack.

7. Play the fool. Your goal is to get your ex to underestimate you. Pretend you are still in love and really do not want to cause him harm. Make him think you want to come back and you can't possibly live without him.

8. Sometimes your ex will be motivated by sheer vindictiveness. When this is what motivates him, he will try to take from you what he perceives that you hold most dear. The trick is to make him think that you are attached to the things that you really do not care about. Convince your ex that you love the cat that keeps peeing on your clothes or some other thing you're not really attached to. That way he will expend his energy trying to take unimportant things from you instead of concentrating on what really matters to you. If you do actually get that damn cat you can

always give it to him or take it to the pound ... what do you care? It pees on your clothes.

9. Play he said-she said. If you can separate your ex from his support group, he will go down a level on Maslow's chart and people become less aggressive if they feel they are alone and have no one to show off for.

10. Try to keep all these strategies going at once. The more different directions you can get your ex to move, the more you will exhaust them while keeping you free from attack. Be careful not to exhaust yourself.

If you over-analyze, it will lead to paralysis. Don't get hung up on the small stuff. If there was ever an important time to stay on task, this is it. Try not to forget that other people have been here too. You are not the only one. Everyone has the divorce story from Hell; why not shoot for having a really great divorce story? Wouldn't it feel good to tell your friends your story and have them laughing by the end of It? Keep in mind that more than half your stuff is on the line. It's worth fighting for it. No one "wins" in divorce, but we want to see you as the one who lost the least. This is a forward motion deal. After the paperwork is filed, it's all just business. Treat it accordingly. Negotiate whatever you can and learn to set your ex up as often as possible. You were married to him so you should know far better than anyone else how to get his goat. This is when it gets good. As soon as you don't give a shit, you'll then have all the power. He who wants the relationship least has all the control. Take it and use it to your advantage.

CHAPTER 11

Methods of Attack

1. If your ex is protecting what is most important to you too well for you to take it from him, then it is usually a good idea to try taking something that is less well defended, but that you have a chance of actually getting. Hopefully, they will move their resources around. If not, take what you can. You can always use it for negotiations later.

2. Getting others to attack your ex. If your ex has been misbehaving, such as having affairs or neglecting to visit the children, or any other thing that his mother would not approve of, tell people about it. Don't whine to people, but tell them what your ex is doing. It is surprising how many people will become self-righteous and be nervy enough to confront your ex about what an ass he is. Trey's friend called his soon-to-be ex-wife to ask her how it felt to be a dead beat mom, who does not pay child support and did not have the common decency to see her children. He even asked her how long she thought it would be before she was knocked up again. The funny part about that was she was already 6 weeks' pregnant with a married man's bastard child. HA-HA!! She was humiliated by the call. BONUS!!

3. If your ex insists on not playing the divorce game and is willing to deal fairly with you without all the games, take the divorce!!

While the game of divorce is fun, it is also time-consuming, expensive, and a hell of a lot of work, so strategically it is always best to end it as soon as possible.

4. Build a support group. Your friends will have ideas on how to play with your ex that will really get under his skin. The most needed thing to remember is to keep up on current events so you don't alienate them with boring and incessant whining. Wait until after the third cocktail before you start plotting with them against the vile ex. This maneuver will assure that you still have friends when your ordeal is over. You won't have to worry about seeing them cringe when you walk in the room.

5. Keep an eye on your ex's life. Always try to attack him when his life has gone topsy-turvy for whatever reason; it may be because he was dumped or maybe he got sick. Whatever it is, try to attack him when he is at his weakest.

6. Find the weakest link in your ex's support system, then get him slobbering drunk and pick his tiny pea brain. Use whatever information you gain and make sure your ex knows exactly where it came from. People who get loose lips while intoxicated will always take themselves and everyone else around them down.

7. If by chance you just cannot seem to get one over on your ex, it means he has already read this book and has learned these lessons much better than you have, and you should just run away! Sorry about your stuff.

GETTING OVER YOUR EX

Dear Trey and Julie,

My wife has left me. I love her so much. I do not know what to do. I cannot help but feel that if I am as nice as I can be, she will eventually see what a great thing she is missing out on. I have been bending over backward trying to please her. I am severely depressed and am not eating.

What can I do?

Soon to be Hot again

Dear Hottie,

You have been rejected by the person you love. She does not want to be with you and have thrown you to the curb like a piece of garbage. OUCH!!! Depression is a natural reaction to this situation. Don't worry, it will pass. One of the best things about depression is that you tend not to eat as much because it is a big hassle to cook and you just do not feel like doing it. However, if you are the type to eat extra crap during depression, throw away all the junk food and buy a pack of Marlboros. This is what the authors have called the divorce diet. It is God's way of making you HOT again. Depression is hard, but the benefit will be worth it. You may also want to get a membership to a gym; you might as well tone while you are losing the weight. Besides, you never know who you may find at the gym.

We also recommend taking on a new lover. This will reaffirm that you are indeed attractive and desirable by the opposite sex. This new lover should be just that, a source of comfort. There should not be any strings attached to this new relationship. You are damaged and broken and are unable to make good decisions concerning the heart at this time. You should be honest with your new lover. Let her know that you do not desire a new relationship, but rather you are looking to satisfy your need for human companionship.

FUN PART OF DIVORCE
Little Annoyances

Divorce is War and Divorce is Love. All's fair in Love and War. What?!? You do not think divorce is love? You say that you hate the person you are divorcing and that is why you are divorcing him? Well, if you truly did not love him, you would not bother with him; you would just leave. All those mean things your ex has done or is doing is because he loves you enough to hate you. Our goal is to kill the love, so that not even an ember of hate remains.

To do this we are going to employ a simple strategy that will convince him that you want an end. Divorce is THE END.

Ha-Ha! This is the best line ever. This one simple line should become your catchphrase. When your ex asks, "Did you change my phone number to an unlisted one and then not tell me what the new number is?" deny it by saying "Oh no! Dear, I would never do anything that mean to you. Not in a million years. HA-HA!" This is now your catchphrase. It is your way of letting him know that you did in fact change his phone number. Who else has access to all the information required to change the number? You know you're caught, he knows you're caught; Ha-Ha is just your way of saying "gottcha!" I did do it but you will never be able to prove it. Not only that, but what I did is LEGAL because I still lived there at the time. HA-HA!!!

CHAPTER 12

Strategies and Situations

Dear Trey and Julie,

My ex and I have finally ended our divorce, but he keeps finding ways to manipulate my life. My ex has told me that he has not given up hope for our relationship and will do whatever it takes to win me back because he loves me!

Just wanna get away

Dear Just Wanna Get Away,

Oh shit, I want my security back. Congratulations, you have been an easy victim. He obviously is not playing with a working strategy like Maslow. Ha-Ha. Remember, you are the cat. Do not kill your mouse, just bat it around and let it think it is winning before you rock its world!!!!!!!!!! Take care of your playthings!!!!! Take what is yours!

There are two ways to deal with this situation. Before you can decide on which method to use, you need to ask yourself this one very simple question: Does he have something you want, or are you done playing with him and are you ready to move on?

If you want something from him, we would suggest that you tell your ex that you do not trust him and you do not believe he is sincere. Then ask for whatever it is you want. Hey, if you're lucky, you might get to fuck with him one last time! HA-HA. Or you can manipulate him for a brutal victimization by sending him to a remedial literacy class for adults. HA-HA. Maybe you can get your Barry Manilow collection back! Who knows, but more important, who cares? The main thing is your ex will do anything within reason to please you!

If you are just plain done with him and just want him to go away, we would suggest scaring him. Remember our advice for sociopaths? It was RUN AWAY!! A friend of ours accomplished this quite by accident. His ex wanted their dog. He really never got along with the animal and the dog and his ex were truly in love. He was going to ask her if she wanted the dog. What pissed him off was that she demanded the dog. So being the evil genius that he is, he decided to mess with her mind. In a stroke of genius he built a shrine to her. He printed out copies of all of their pictures, put them in frames, set candles around them, and he took out all of the love letters she had written him over the years. He even went so far as to frame his favorites. He set everything up in a semi-circle, then waited for her to arrive! When she arrived at his house all by herself, he begged her to come in and chat with him a little. The poor fool agreed, so he very cheerfully led her by the hand to the center of the semi-circle that he had prepared for her. Once she was comfortably situated with a drink in her hand, he proceeded to tell her how he could not get her out of his mind—thinking about her night and day. He even made up some really messed up dreams that were so bad that even Hannibal Lector would say, "My God that dude is fucking NUTS!!"

The soon-to-be ex-wife listened a lot more patiently than what our friend was expecting. She eventually told him that he needed to seek psychiatric help, and that she really needed to get going. As she was leaving, he asked her for a lock of her hair, but refused to tell her why he wanted it. She very quickly loaded the dog up in the car and left his home and his life. The very next day our friend got a call from his attorney saying that his soon-to-be ex signed the divorce decree, and she has chosen not to take anything from the marriage. That was the last time he ever saw her! HA-HA. Have a nice life in Qua-Quaville.

She did tell everyone about the shrine and, of course, our friend denied it! Our friend is a kind, shy little guy. No one believed her when she claimed he was crazy and advised people to keep their distance from him. The more she insisted that he was dangerous and psychotic, the crazier she looked. HA-HA. It has been 11 years since he pulled this little prank on her. Our friend swears up and down that she is the greatest ex that he has ever had!! She just left and did not even attempt to take any of his stuff, other than the dog. Who could ask for more from an ex?

Booby Trap

Booby traps are a bad idea. If your ex is breaking into your house, make your house secure. Change the locks and lock the windows. Tell your neighbors that if they see your ex to call the police. If your ex gets hurt and can prove that you intentionally left a booby trap for him, you can be sued. It does not matter that he was trespassing when he hurt himself.

When Kelly was going through his divorce, his ex would climb in through a window to go snooping through his stuff trying to learn if he was seeing anyone or not. So Kelly took a board, hammered some nails into it and set it under the window she was using to gain access. Unfortunately Kelly forgot about his booby trap when he locked his keys in the house! Yep, poor Kelly wound up with three nails in his foot and a tetanus shot. What a boob!! The good news is that Kelly's ex did not fall into his booby trap; otherwise, he would have been sued to high heaven and lost all of his stuff!

Journals and Documentation

We can't stress enough the importance of documentation. As dear old Dad has drilled into our head forever, DOCUMENT, DOCUMENT,

DOCUMENT!! The fine art of documentation can and must be utilized correctly! Your journal will be taken as evidence in a court of law. It doesn't matter if it is on a bar napkin, it counts. You need to write times and dates as well as feelings and perceptions. Always write from the perspective of the victim. If you happen to be a large man divorcing a petite woman, be scared of her friends. Make sure to include places and even imagined slights. Hopefully, your ex will be ignorant and lazy so you will be the only voice that the judge hears. HA-HA.

Picture Taking

The funniest part of going through a divorce is that your ex will tell you how to best annoy him. One day while Trey and his ex were at the marriage counselor, his ex very politely asked him to stop taking pictures of her and her friends. What?!?!?

Of course, he denied doing it as he grinned as wide as he could. It was the equivalent of saying Ha-Ha in a way that did not make him look bad in front of the marriage counselor. He honestly had not taken any pictures of her or her friends. Why would he? He did start taking pictures the very next day! It was amazing how such a little harmless action sent her through the roof! He never would have thought of taking pictures of the ex's friends or even his own. He started carrying a disposable camera with him at all times because he never knew when he would bump into them, while they were shopping, or at the bar, or wherever. Gosh darn it!! He got caught taking their picture every single time. We guess yelling "smile" as you take a picture is not a very good way of being inconspicuous! It is also fun if you do have to go through a face-to-face argument to snap a picture of them every time they start yelling! These pictures are also great for the divorce party.

Another big bonus to picture taking is to stoke your ex's paranoia to an all-time high. This will knock him completely off kilter, which is where you want him to be if you are going to come out on top in the long run. Eventually, when he starts screaming at you about the camera he thinks you have, you can tape him in secret and really get some good stuff. The judge and shrink will appreciate the extra effort on your part to show how truly crazy your ex has become. Ha-Ha.

Imaginary Car Damage

Your ex will tell all kinds of lies to his friends and your friends. The one action that Trey's ex did that really got under his skin was accusing him of damaging her car. She did not accuse him of breaking a headlight, cracking her windshield, or even flattening her tires. All of these things he could have accomplished. What she accused him of were things like draining the oil out of her car or taking the seals out of the transmission. Our personal favorite was breaking her drive line. Keep in mind that Trey would actually purchase blinker fluid if he thought it would prolong the life of his bulbs because he can't change those either. The reason this got under his skin so badly is because she was the person who showed him where to put oil in his own car. When it comes to cars, he is totally clueless. He can change a flat but other than that, he has to take it to a mechanic or to Julie to have it fixed.

One day his friend asked him if he really broke his ex's drive line. He said, "Her drive line is broken?" HA-HA! After his friend left he asked Julie what the hell a drive line is. They went and crawled under Julie's car and she pointed to this HUGE pipe thing that goes from the back to the front of a car. As they lay underneath the car, he asked Julie how the hell you could break one of those. She started laughing at his ignorance and pointed out that his ex's car is a front wheel drive so it doesn't even have a drive line. HE WAS PISSED!! Ok, damn it bitch, you got him on that one. To make matters worse, Julie reminds him of it every chance she gets!! She gets a lot of those chances.

Junk Mail

This little stunt was never done to one of our ex's. It was actually done to a good friend of ours named Rob Dutton. Rob, Julie, and

Trey celebrate April Fool's day for an entire month. We have done this since high school. Rob had moved to another city so it was not easy to pull a prank on him, but we managed. We hopped on the Internet and did a keyword search for "Free Catalogs." We filled out the forms with our names and his address and telephone number. We put our names on it so that he would know that we got him! About a month later he called us up to tell us that we have got to stop sending him catalogs. We acted shocked, "You mean you do not need a catalog of women's clothing? What about the one for industrial rubber supply? Surely you used that one. What about the catalog of sex toys?" He denied ordering anything from that one, but we know better!

Well apparently he did not need any of those catalogs, but every day when he got home his mailbox was crammed full of the junk. It was causing him a lot of grief because we sent him over 700 different catalogs. It is amazing how many times you can point and click in an hour or two. Eventually, the post office quit delivering his mail. He had to make special arrangements to pick it up. We had no idea that it would cause him that big of a problem. We were just trying to be a little bit funny, not totally annoying!! Sorry Rob! Now if you wanted to annoy your ex, what a great way to do it. Not only that but he will never be able to prove you did it so long as you do not put your name on the catalog. Your ex will know damn well it was you! Without proof, there is nothing they can do about it. You should use a very creative pseudonym like Corey B. Itch

You can also sign him up for hate groups! Then he can get phone calls and other information sent to them. Give these people your piece-of-shit ex's address and phone number. Just a subtle little way of letting your ex know what you really think of him walking out on your family. All of this information is easily found on the Internet! All you have to do is a keyword search for hate group or hate watch. Sign him up for as many as you can. Send the group's e-mails requesting information to be sent to your ex's address! Call the group up and tell them that you would like to host a meeting. Give them your ex's work phone number. Of course, harassing your ex in this manner is illegal and we do not recommend doing this, but then again, how is your ex going to prove it?

Another highly recommended strategy is to show considerable concern for their immortal souls. This is a really great way to help keep Mormons, Jehovah Witnesses, and Kirby salesmen off your porch. How could your ex be pissed when you're looking after their eternal souls and their carpet? Who is going to bitch about being on every prayer list from here to eternity?

Correspondence

When receiving correspondence from your ex, it is best to ignore as much of it as you can. But there are a few simple procedures to follow when receiving this form of communication. Before you do anything to the letter, photocopy it. You may need it later in the courtroom. Once the photocopying is done, it is red pen time. That's right, break out your old English book and start correcting his letter. Be brutal with the corrections.

If you are not good at English, take it to someone who is and have him or her help you correct the letter. Put plenty of snide comments that are irrelevant to your court case in the margins, things such as "I cannot believe you think you should be in charge of our child's education. I think our 12-year-old has better command of the English language than you do," or how about "Did you really graduate high school?" You can even be helpful in your insult by writing something like, "My God, I had no idea you were this illiterate. You know there are classes for illiterate adults. Maybe you should go." They may even meet our good friend Dick there!!

If the letter is from their attorney and you have BALLS OF STEEL, correct their letter too! Wouldn't it be hilarious to challenge their lack of command with the English language? How much fun would it be to remind your ex's attorney that it is a good thing that the bar exam was multiple guess because if there were an essay portion there would have been no way in hell he or she would have ever gotten a license to practice. The real reason attorneys use legalese is because the rest of us don't know what the hell they're talking about.

So go ahead and do it! Nothing is more gratifying than breaking out the trusty old red sharpie and don't forget to give it a letter grade! It is important that you photocopy it first for your records and then return the corrected original to your ex.

These are fun to deliver by hand, as the look on their face is priceless. You get to laugh and you do not have to worry about running into the graded correspondence in court. Who in their right mind would look a judge in the eye and complain about that? That will shut them up. If you are the type who just has to write a letter to your ex, do it on a computer and don't e-mail it to them, just give it to them. That way if the correspondence should show up somewhere, you can deny writing it.

If you have the great fortune to receive a handwritten letter or note from your ex, hang on to it as these are priceless. Hopefully, they are completely incoherent and rambling, as handwritten notes usually are. If you are really lucky, he will write you a long and rambling letter begging to come home or to return some stuff he didn't bother to take with him. Again be sure and grade this ruthlessly. Consult your old high school English teacher if necessary. Hell, she's probably retired and could use a good laugh. Take this amazing opportunity to demean your ex and don't forget to save a copy for your divorce party. If he is upset enough to pen you a personal note, then he still cares, which gives you the upper hand. You'll never have a graded piece of correspondence thrown back in your face because people hate to have their ignorance pointed out in red pen.

Computer

Hopefully, you shared the computer with your ex. After he is gone, it is imperative that you find a computer geek and have your hard drive combed over for any incriminating evidence. This will come in handy for threats and blackmail. Even if there is nothing there, it's a good idea to say there was. After all, who has the computer? It's up to him to prove his innocence. You can look at him straight in the face and say, "Why were you on the (pick their fetish) website? You're one sick puppy." Then go tell his family what he was doing online. He'll never be looked at the same way again. Don't forget to forward everything to interested parties such as Mom or clergy.

Remember that in this age of incredible technology there is no reason that you should ever actually speak to your ex. You can e-mail, text, or simply pin a note to your kid's lapel. A few months of not speaking to that shrieking shrew should cure your migraines forever.

CHAPTER 13

Fun Stories: What to Do & Not to Do

"PEOPLE THINK ABOUT DIVORCE FOR 18 MONTHS" IS WHAT HIS ATTORNEY TOLD him. What kind of masochist has that kind of patience? If you're not happy, you're never going to be happy. All the time in the world can pass and you'll still be married to Lucifer with PMS, coupled with a hell of a case of blue balls. Be aware when they are nice to you, it is no good. Remember that this too will pass. Our education reminds us that hindsight is 20/20.

Let's take a look at Luke. He is a highly charismatic, articulate, and handsome man. This man is very intelligent, well traveled, and highly educated. He also has hideous taste in women; he married the antichrist. It will happen to the best of us; however, we should remember to tread lightly and never make eye contact, or turn our backs once we have realized the error of our ways. This type of spouse makes Cujo look like Lassie.

In his infinite wisdom, he divorced the same woman not once, not twice, but three times. This guy is a glutton for punishment. However handsome and well educated he may be, he has issues dealing with reality.

Luke had the unfortunate position of divorcing the typical psychopath. In fact, they used to be neighbors with Dick and Jane. Vanessa and Jane are interchangeable. The million dollar question is why do these men seem to be addicted to mentally ill women who torture them and destroy their families relentlessly with no remorse? Trey, Dick, and Luke seem to be obsessed with horrible women. Julie is still wondering if the pussy is fur-lined or gold-plated. She can't understand why these educated and otherwise intelligent men insist on torturing themselves over these poisonous individuals. They can't seem to move past the fact that these women are Oscar-worthy actresses who will lie, cheat, and do whatever evil that will get them what they want right now. If a woman is unwilling to make her family her first priority, then she is junk and should be put out with the rest of the rubbish. If you are one of these guys who has the misfortune to pick one of these women for your partner, you need to accept the fact that you were lied to and take action. Get over it. She sucks and you're better off alone than with the drama and bullshit that such women will inevitably bring into your life. Once you're Ok with being alone, good things will start to happen.

The problem that Luke encounters is that he is trying to do the right thing. He is actually concerned about his children and can't seem to move on. He consistently mourns the loss of his family, which is the normal thing to do. He fights with his ex over every inconsequential thing. This is an insidious form of control that the ex-from-hell exercises. The only thing you can do is to recognize it and treat it accordingly. The most effective way to deal with these folks is to pick your battles. If it's not a big deal let them think that they have won. Won what? It doesn't really matter. As long as you let them think that they are in control, you win. Pick your battles with these guys or gals. They are easily manipulated as they aren't too bright and can't really see the big picture.

The problem this presents you is that as long as you're angry, they still have control in your life. You cannot move on to be with someone else or even enjoy peace in your own life as long as your ex, still has the ability to raise any kind of emotion in you. Remember, emotion is the enemy. Business is business. End of report. When dealing with your ex keep in mind that it is no different than an estate in probate. It signifies the death of your marriage.

Everything is just business and you can get more bees with honey than vinegar. As long as you keep emotion at bay, you will be better off. Get over it. Get on to the good stuff that allows you control over your own destiny. Keep in mind as you are bickering and squabbling with your ex, you're really costing yourself time from your new life. Hopefully, you'll be able to learn whatever lesson you were supposed to. Then just remember that you don't want to do that again and find someone who adores you and treats you accordingly. Or get yourself a nice dog. "Alone" is not a dirty word. It's better to be alone and be lonesome than with someone that makes you feel like shit. It's important to know yourself and not mind spending time with yourself. When it all boils down, you are the only one you have to live with. As long as you can look at yourself in the mirror and not be completely repulsed, you're doing Ok.

Luke dropped the ball in his divorce because he forgot to play the victim. He was set up perfectly for it. He could have just said "bullshit." He, however, took the high road, usually your first mistake. He should have called her cheating, lying ass as he saw it. He eventually wound up with the house and everything else that counts. But putting himself through three divorces from the same woman is a bit more than it should have taken. Maybe sometimes it just takes a little longer to gloat. Checkmate!

One very simple exercise you can practice is remembering to keep your voice at an all-time low. We all had parents, right? Think back to when they were screaming at you about missing curfew, stealing the car, or whatever. We don't know about you, but we didn't hear a word they said; they just said a lot of them. On the other hand, when our best friends were whispering a particularly juicy bit of gossip in our ear, we strained to hear every syllable.

Your ex is exactly the same way. Next time your ex is pushing your buttons trying to get you to sink to his level, say very quietly that you would like to continue this conversation at a later date when he is able to control himself and not behave like a child. You win. Ha-Ha.

No one deserves to be screamed at. The ironic thing is that the one doing the screaming is the one who comes off as the asshole.

Don't let him make you yell and ignore him while he is shrieking at you. All it takes is a bit of training and everyone will be better off for it.

When you accidentally run into your ex in public, a good way to deal with it is to pretend that you've never met. You can usually accomplish this by putting on a blank face and calling him by someone else's name, preferably an ex-lover that he was really jealous of. It goes something like this: "Oh hey, Steve, long-time no see. How the hell have you been?"

This will accomplish a couple of things. You'll let him know that he no longer has a spot in your heart, and you no longer even think of him. You win and you don't even have to spend any money.

We're always at our best when we're in love and happy. The hard part is finding someone who loves us back. It's important to realize that it's not always possible to be with someone else. It gets really boring and redundant to be alone all the time; however, when you do meet someone else it's worth it. In the meantime, there are always good books and cable TV. Don't forget your dog.

Please have standards. People will lower their standards just to avoid being alone. This will do nothing but bring you heartache. If you're settling just so you don't have to sleep alone, you're missing the entire point of living. While you're sleeping with that person who is definitely not the "one," you are doing yourself a huge disservice. The "one" might be next door, but you won't notice because you're busy wasting your time on an idiot who is just filling space because you're lonesome. Better to be strong and alone than to throw yourself under the bus because you don't want to be solo. That's nonsense. You may choose to be alone, but you are never really alone. There are people who will tolerate your company because they're lonesome too. You may choose to utilize these people, but keep in mind that they will never really grow into being the "one." There is nothing wrong with spending time and commiserating with these folks as long as everyone understands that there will never really be anything else. A good idea is to find people who live differently from you and have very high moral standards. Look for people who have it worse than you, but seem to be inexplicably happy anyway. Volunteering at a homeless shelter or battered women's shelter is a good idea. Identify where your strong suits are and try to help people who have it worse than you. It is very therapeutic for everyone involved. The most important thing to do is remove the negative. If it makes you feel bad, don't do it. Even if everyone else tells you it should be fun but you still have a twinge of guilt, don't do it. Go to church or the beach, mountains, or anywhere that puts your soul at peace.

Learn to take joy in the small things in life. It may be something as simple as the phone not ringing. It may be a particularly spicy episode of Jerry Springer. Everyone has something to find joy in, no matter how mundane it may be. You just need to find your happy place. Stop blaming your ex for your misery. That's just one more way he has control over you. The best thing to do is just to let it go. It's easier said than done. If the 12-step program we suggested doesn't appeal to you, we have many more suggestions. Go to the gym, take yoga, learn a foreign language, read a good book. Hell, write a good book. Whatever you decide to put your effort into, it has to be just for you and no one else. Some of us play billiards, ride motorcycles, or build classic cars. As long as your new-found passion doesn't involve the opposite sex, you'll be better off. Your heart and soul needs to heal. You're the only one who can decide how long your mourning period should be. Everyone is different. We're not really endorsing any time frame; everyone will know his or her own. Trey will lie in bed for 6 months and wallow or organize one of his many collections. Julie has a bonfire, hits the clubs, and spends the next 6 months hung over. Our friend Shannon took years and actually worked on her house. We're all over it. As for our other friends, they are taking a lot longer. We don't know why this is. Some lash out in anger, others just act like hermits and disappear for weeks on end. Is it because some of us are capable of loving better than others, or are they just better at being miserable?

We are all capable of controlling our own behaviors. You have the choice to decide if you're going to act like everything is all right, especially when it's not. Or are you going to hang on forever and keep things not all right? There is much to be said about keeping a stiff upper lip. What came first, the chicken or the egg? What do you choose, a few good times or mourning forever—especially on the days you can't imagine getting out of bed. What do you decide? If you get out of bed, it will hurt like hell for the first little bit. Then pretty soon you'll be distracted and forget about what hurts. Even if it's just for a few hours it's a break from your self-imposed misery. Look at it like this: You can always go back to bed and wallow, it's not going anywhere. However, the event you found that looks kind of like fun will be over in a few hours. Not every time you leave the house will be enjoyable. In fact, some of them will be downright miserable. You may run into people you hoped you'd never see again. You may spill something and ruin your favorite pair of pants. Hell, you may even wreck your car. But all that stuff is just life, get over it, and get on with it.

But on other days, you may need to check and make sure it's really you. Sometimes really good things happen, but if you choose to stay in bed, you may miss them. Check your horoscope.

CHAPTER 14

How to Host a Suicide

THIS IS A VERY IMPORTANT THING TO DO. REMEMBER YOU HAVE JUST BEEN through hell and now you are done. This is your last parting shot. This is the metaphorical equivalent of taking a sling shot loaded with Ha-Ha and aiming at your ex's ass ... then letting it rip. Don't forget to leave a mark. Celebration is a must. You are officially declaring yourself the winner!

Your celebration should include lots of liquor, drunken friends, and games. Good games will require the worst picture you can find of your ex. Then hit the xerox machine and blow that bitch up to life-sized posters; you'll need more than one. If you don't have a suitably embarrassing one of your ex, then get on the computer and electronically alter one yourself. You can superimpose his head on a donkey if you like. This is why God invented fetish porn sights. If you had the foresight to videotape any psychotic episodes, bring those too. High-definition plasma is a wonderful thing. You can play these videos over and over all night long to remind yourself how truly fortunate you are and give your friends lots of giggles. If you have any naked pictures or homemade porn, those can be fun too.

We highly recommend inviting your ex but tell him about 2 hours later than everybody else. That way everyone is liquored up for the roast. If you've followed our advice your ex is thoroughly qua-quaed and is so hungry for any morsel of acceptance he should be dumb enough to actually show up. After all, this is his divorce too. Explain to him that it is important for your "mutual" friends to see that everyone has moved on and there is no need to be childish and petty.

Some of our favorite childish and petty games to play at a divorce party are darts; of course, the dart board is a cut-out of the ex's face. Remember the darts should be put away before your ex arrives. Dangerous, sharp stuff sucks. You may also try playing pin the (penis/vagina) on the horrid vile ex. You should always pin the pricks on your ex-husband and the puss on your ex-wife. Keep in mind that challenging their heterosexuality forever is your right. After all, who would be dumb enough to divorce the best fuck on the planet? There are many games that can be played at this kind of event. Think back to the drinking games you played in high school and try to apply them to this situation.

Everyone likes to gamble. Why should your ex be immune? Have everyone throw in a few bucks and start a pool on when the stupid ex will remarry, get knocked up, or catch a social disease. Don't forget the poster boards as they will need to be large and easy to read.

Love letters can be turned into drinking games. Never throw away a mushy love letter. It can be used for years and years. You never know when your ex may decide to run for office. In the meantime, you and your friends can bust out a bottle and take a shot every time your ex was stupid enough to record that bullshit. Simply photocopy that sucker and hand it out.

Everyone loves to share their memories and advice. Simply hang a blank poster board that sports a picture of your ex's head over a mammal silhouette. Then take some sharpies and encourage your guests to record their favorite memory of your ex. This makes a great keepsake, but you don't want your kids to see it until after you are dead.

Location, Location, Location. Unless you desperately need new carpet and don't like your stuff anymore you should never, ever plan this at your house. This little soiree needs to be on neutral ground. Find a local pub or church basement that has a private room that you can sneak booze into pretty easily. If you can get back into the basement of the church you were married in—awesome. This is the definition of irony at its finest. You'll have come full circle. Ha-Ha.

When your ex arrives, he will see a physical manifestation of your innermost deepest feelings of him. Coach your friends to point their fingers and yell Ha-Ha. This is ten times better than any lame-ass surprise party you've ever planned. If your ex has harbored secret fantasies about coming home, this will squash those forever with a side dish of humiliation. Hell, you'll have done him a favor as now their shrink will have something to work with. It's important to get your money out of therapy and give your Mom a fuck'n break already, will ya?

Congratulations, you have won! Now all you have left to do is sit back and think of all the fun times you had making your ex feel stupid, pathetic, and played. My God, who would have thought that divorce could be so much fun. I know you cannot wait to do it all over again with a brand new victim to QUA-QUASH under your boot of HA-HA. How does it feel to be the Ha-Ha ex? Tell us, how did you do it?

Glossary

Adultery—What the shit-head spouse usually commits. Unfortunately, it is no longer a crime unless you are actively serving in a branch of the Armed forces. Even then you have to screw your commanding officer's spouse. The acceptance of screwing around on marriage vows is a big reason we have many of the problems we do. Where is the shame?

Alimony—(palimony, spousal support): What you have to pay if you are a complete idiot. You may be the sole supporting spouse and it sucks when you are forced to give it to the idiot who probably screwed around on you **and made it all your fault and has shown absolutely no remorse.**

Child Support—If you are not the custodial parent this is what you are required to pay. If you don't, you are a dirt bag.

Creative Silence—Another term for blackmail. If it works to your best advantage to keep silent about an indiscretion that your ex may have committed then do so, for the right price. How nice of you to keep your ex's secrets even when he has been so mean to you. You saint you.

Custodial Parent—The parent who doesn't have to pay child support. Hopefully, it is the same parent who has the child's best interest in mind and isn't a petty asshole.

The Defendant—Hopefully, what you are not. This means you were too late to sue for divorce first. Unless you pull it together fast, you may be headed to Qua-Quaville.

Guardian ad Litem—Someone you pay to represent your child or children in a court of law. Usually an out-of-work social worker, or a retired English teacher. Not good for you or your children.

Ha-Ha—What you do want to be. They have no pride, no dignity. They are unpredictable and are not to be trusted. They take glee in their ex-spouse's demise and keep all the stuff. They have been known to write books that rake their already decimated ex's ass over the coals. Ha-Ha.

Immoral Honesty—If you are being creatively silent about some indiscretion that your ex has committed in the past. When he refuses to meet your demands, then honesty is the best policy. Remember, it is not your fault that his actions have natural consequences. Tell as many people as you can. HA-HA.

Mediator—The person you pay an obscene hourly wage to fuck you over. This makes the court happy because they will probably not have to hear your case if you get screwed here instead of in the actual courtroom.

Mental Illness—What you need to instill in your ex if he didn't come with one already.

Order of Protection—Something, hopefully, you got before your soon-to-be-ex did.

The Plaintiff—What you should be if you were on the ball in the whole game of divorce. It basically means you sued first, well done. You've set yourself up to be the Ha-Ha.

Qua-Qua—What you don't want to be. Victimized but keeping their head high and pride intact while being fucked in the ass. Qua-Qua's are usually very noble and lose all their stuff.

Restraining Order—Also, something you should've gotten before your soon-to-be-ex did.

Temporary Custody—What you will automatically be awarded if you are the first one at the courthouse. It will stick until you can get in front of the judge. If you are fortunate enough to live in a small town or a town that has a terribly overworked justice system, this can buy you up to a year to decimate your ex and by that time custody will be yours.

Acknowledgments

Ross Barnette, for pointing us in the right direction. Diane Collins, for editing and being the original Ha-Ha. Shannon Sin, for free counseling. Connie Miller, for hours and hours of drunken giggling and inspiration (we would love to actually meet you sometime). Aunt Lynnette, for being a pioneer in smart and single living. Marc Collins for unwavering love and support. Frank Gambino, for honest opinions and lots of loud laughter. Louis Collins, for actually believing this was possible. We also want to acknowledge our children, Taylor "Slick" Herron, Paige Herron, and Sidney V. Anderson IV. We love and adore you and will try our best not to fuck you up too bad. Our support team that tolerates our neurosis; we're sorry, we love you all lots. Miriam Rich, Kris Dvarskis, Sid and Edena Anderson, Gavin Williams, Chris Lenihan, Troy Thiel, Cher and Mike Ross, Bob Houghtailing, Cherie and Terry Williams, Connie and Myron Bryant, Dave Morris, Kirt Koski, Greg Loomis, Holly Norgard, Kevin Tate, John Dines, Launa Ogden, Kate and Dave Morgan, Kenny Hack, Melanie and John Rudell, Miki and Tom Caspillo, Pat and Scott Burton, Sandy Kellogg, Cindy Brachtenbach, Kyle Dietz, Rob Dutton, Troy Bray, and finally, Tye and Tabitha Herron.

Inspiration

We would like to thank the following people for inspiring us. They have stomped our guts in the ground and ruined our faith in humanity, making the writing of this book possible and necessary.

Saundra M. Schoenhardt, Chrissy Latimer, Richard Miller, last and certainly least, Mary Lyons.

If you were not mentioned in the inspiration list don't worry about it, you didn't count anyway.

 One special note: To the "Narcissist," we know who you are and you know who you are, but no one else does. HA-HA.

About the Authors

Trey Anderson

Sidney Vincent Anderson III (Trey) is the product of generations of honorable men and women. They have married their high school and college sweethearts and they have actually stayed married to them until death. Trey is the first divorce that his family has suffered on either side of his family in four generations of matrimonial bliss.

We thought he was a pioneer, but it turns out that Trey suffers from a recessive gene problem. It is referred to as "knight in shining armor." It is a horrible affliction and explains his hideous taste in women. His family was not aware that it carried this malady and have scientists working around the clock to identify and isolate this gene so, hopefully, it can be eradicated for future generations.

Even though Trey's marriages ended in disaster, he has upheld his most important requirement for the family tree. He has produced a male heir, Sidney Vincent Anderson IV. We have decided that, due to this wonderful child, Trey's fateful unions were not a complete waste of time. He retains custody of his son and resides in Casper, Wyoming. He currently attends the University of Wyoming at Casper and will be an elementary teacher when he is done (some people never learn).

Julie Collins

Trey and Julie have been best friends since the fifth grade. Unfortunately in the seventh grade Julie, who was raised under power lines, sprouted to the great height of 6 feet, while Trey maintained the dwarfish height of 5 feet two inches. Ever since then they have been dubbed Boris and Natasha. Their families have known and worked together for four generations, so this collaboration was inevitable.

For as unblemished as Trey's family history is, Julie comes by her divorces as a rite of passage. She is the product of one of the most dysfunctional families on the planet. Both of her parents are attractive people, who had no business having children. Julie's family has been riddled with divorce from the beginning of time, probably due to the foul disposition of the females involved. If they are related to Julie and haven't divorced, they should. She isn't real sure what a good marriage is supposed to look like, since Trey's parents, Sid and Edena Anderson, and John and Melanie Rudell, are the only examples she has ever had. Sid and Edena moved to Saudi Arabia 15 years ago; John and Melanie moved to Colorado as soon as they figured out that Julie was indeed going to be a permanent fixture in their home unless they left the state immediately.

Julie resides in Casper, Wyoming, with her two teenaged children, Taylor and Paige, and her St. Bernard, Sweet Marc, whom she adores. She enjoys working on her cars, playing pool, and political debates with liberals. She is currently dating and has no plans of settling down; in fact, has decided to revert to her youth as soon as the kids move out.

She is currently an independent financial adviser, which isn't sexy but it pays the bills. There's not a huge job market for mermaids in Wyoming so she had to settle in the career department, but has learned the hard way that "settling" in the mate department isn't an option.

Louis Collins
RIP 12/12/1943–07/04/2009

The Illustrator of *How To Make Divorce Fun* was Julie's father Louis Collins. Louie was a prime example of what happens to children who are the product of divorce. He had six sets of parents growing up and that should explain his rather jaded outlook on the "family scene." Louie lived in Las Vegas, Nevada, where he built hot rods and played pool for fun. He appreciated fine Scotch and strippers and never had to revert back to his youth, due to the fact that he never aged much past the age of 19.